Project Lifecycles

How to Reduce Risks, Release
Successful Products, and Increase
Agility

Johanna Rothman

Project Lifecycles

How to Reduce Risks, Release Successful Products, and Increase Agility

Johanna Rothman

Practical **ink**

© Johanna Rothman. This book is available in these formats: Ebook: 978-1-943487-31-8; Paper: 978-1-943487-32-5; Hardcover: 978-1-943487-33-2

To Mark and the rest of our family, as always.

Contents

Praise Quotes

this book offers it in spades!" —Jay Hrcsko, Agile Transformation Director, Agile Uprising Podcast host

"An essential read for anyone seeking to navigate the complexities of project risks and feedback loops, ensuring teams can deliver value rapidly and sustainably. Rothman's expertise shines through, offering a practical guide to transforming your project approach, avoiding the pitfalls of 'fake agility,' and embracing a culture of flow to drive successful, customer-centric outcomes." —Heidi Araya, Director of Engineering Operations & Program Manager

"A comprehensive and nuanced taxonomy of ways to structure projects, including success preconditions, failure modes, and trade-offs. Pragmatic as ever, Johanna offers advice from experience tailored to a variety of contexts. Be honest with yourself about yours and this book will take you far." —Amitai Schleier, experienced technical leader & host of the Agile in 3 Minutes podcast

"*Project Lifecycles* is a guiding light, offering practical tips to improve value delivery. A must-read for those who aspire to not just adopt agile, but truly understand and embody agility in their professional journey. —Leland Newsom, Enterprise Agile Coach

"Everyone cares about good products. If you feel stuck in an ineffective product development approach, this book will give you the arguments you need to make change. Johanna Rothman's extensive, practical experience of project lifecycles will help you reduce risks, make good decisions, and respond to feedback. You'll understand why and how to do better." —April Johnson, catalyst for collective change

"A brilliant approach to rethinking the strengths, weaknesses and applicability of various project lifecycles. Learn the right questions to ask about your project's goals and risks, so that you can select the right lifecycle for your project and team. An absolute must-read for all software professionals." —Jenny Dormoy, Seasoned Technical Program Manager and Leader

Acknowledgments

I thank all my blog readers who said, "Ooh, we have choices." I also thank my clients, especially those who wanted "their" agile approach.

I thank Mark Posey for his editing. I thank Cathi Stevenson for her cover design.

Cover image by Pixelsaway/Depositphotos.com

Any mistakes are mine.

Preface

A colleague called me and asked, "Is it reasonable to take agile training all online?"

I said, "As long as your team is taking the training with you, sure. Especially if you're part of a distributed team. You don't need to be all in one place to have a successful agile team."

"No," he said. "You don't get it. I'm taking 'training' by watching videos. Myself. Just me and my computer. There's no training. I'm just watching. And I'll get a certificate at the end!"

I'm sure I swore or something equally useful as a response. But this guy's a character, so I thought I'd check. "You're not teasing me, are you?"

"No, I'm not. I'm totally for real."

I asked several questions about the principles behind his training and learned that the trainers had dressed up a waterfall approach to look like a well-known agile approach. There was no idea about cross-functional teams. No learning about the product and the process. And not enough emphasis on defining and delivering value to a customer on a regular basis.

Worse, there was little to no emphasis on the customer's experience once they received an increment of value. That meant they had little to no useful feedback about the product as they developed it.

This is fake agility, agile-in-name-only. And that's what my colleague was being "taught." (I hesitate to say he learned anything at all useful.)

Fake agility is why people rant about agility and demand to return to a waterfall. (They haven't really left the waterfall.) It's also why people want to work alone, so they can manage their careers.

Agile approaches don't have to be like that. Worse, we shouldn't call these ideas agile anything. We can call them by the names they deserve, which is the lifecycle name.

If you suspect you have fake agility where you work, consider the ideas in this book to learn what you're doing and make it better. You can create a more agile culture in your project and for your product that will work better than anything dressed in fake agile clothing.

And if you persist, you might be able to influence your manager to start creating a better product development culture, regardless of whether it's real or fake agility.

Use this book to see and experiment with more ideas about how to manage your projects, create products your customers enjoy using, and create a better culture for success. Regardless of your lifecycle.

Johanna Rothman

Arlington, Massachusetts

List of Figures

Chapter 1. The Shameful Secret: Fake Agility is the Norm

The lifecycle wars have been fought, and "agile" has won. Right?

I wish that were true. If "agile" had won these wars, these statements would be true:

- All teams are cross-functional, with all the skills the team needs to discover the actual requirements and deliver a product the customers love.
- No team has to plan for more than a month or so because everyone expects to adapt the plan based on customer feedback of interim deliverables.
- Managers focus on creating an environment that enables and rewards collaborative teams, not the effort of any specific individual.

Instead, every week or two, I read a blog post somewhere about how "agile" is terrible. That's because many organizations use a two-week iteration as a death march for the team. The teams rightly feel they must deliver a finished product every two weeks. And they don't have time to think about and make critical decisions, such as for the UI or the architecture.

Worse, because teams are in a death march, they don't have time to integrate customer feedback into their product development. And don't get me started on trying to measure individual "productivity" or "velocity."

None of that is an agile approach. It's jamming traditional, control-based thinking into "agile" ideas—the proverbial square peg into a round hole. No wonder people think "agile" is a bad word. That's agility in name, not in action.

"Agile" is an Adjective

Many people have shortened "The Agile Manifesto for Software Development" to the word "Agile." But notice that the word is an adjective that describes an approach or a technique. Not a noun.

It's even worse when someone says, "Agile/Scrum" because they think Scrum is the only agile approach.

Instead, I will use agility because that word describes a property of nimbleness. Or, I'll use agile as an adjective, to describe a team or a culture. I hope you decide to consider this usage, too.

But teams aren't the only ones who pay for fake agility. So do first-level, and middle managers. And, too often, senior managers do, too.

How is this possible? Because while people in the organization change their practices, no one changes the culture.

Real agility—not fake agility—requires a culture of agility at all levels. Let's start with what an agile team culture might look like.

1.1. Visualize a Successful Agile Team Culture

An agile team culture means the cross-functional team delivers useful value often. Then, the team obtains and uses customer feedback to choose what to do next and how. In addition, the team reflects on how they worked and what they want to change for the next increment of value.

Just as important, the team has the autonomy to work the way they want to. That means no one assigns work to any particular person on the team. The team members decide how to best work, as individuals and as a team.

In addition, the team decides how to organize their work, often with some kind of a board. I've seen many kinds of team boards: on corkboards, on whiteboards, with many columns or just three columns. Even if the team has a facilitative leader, that leader does not tell the team what their board should look like.

The team always gets to choose how they work.

However, an agile team has a product leader, who, with the team's perspective, decides what is most important for the team to do next. That product leader ranks the work, so everyone knows what work is first, second, and third. Even better, the team knows what they don't have to do yet. The team might need a look-ahead to keep their design options open, but the team finishes the immediate work and waits to start the future work.

In a real sense, the team keeps these two questions in mind as they develop the product:

- How do we maintain technical excellence on the current work so we can demonstrate and then receive feedback from customers or internal people?
- How do we make future changes easier?

There is no control function, such as a manager, inside an agile team—unless the team members want that function. Most successful agile teams I see do need someone to facilitate the team's decisions and to protect the team from other people's multitasking requests. In addition, if the team is missing some necessary capabilities or skills, sometimes that team needs a cross-organization negotiator to hire or obtain those people from other teams.

(I call that facilitator and negotiator an agile project manager—because that person creates a better agile environment for the team.)

The multitasking requests or insufficient staffing most often occur when the product leaders and management are still discovering how to work in an agile way.

That's why an agile team culture is not enough. The teams and the organization also need an agile product culture.

1.2. Visualize a Successful Agile Product Culture

In traditional organizations, a product manager, often with the help of business analysts, writes a requirements document at the start of the project. Sometimes, those documents take months to write.

However, an agile product culture defines the product strategy, and the product goal, often within a day. Then the product leader asks this question: What is the smallest chunk of value I want the customers to see as soon as possible?

That means agile product leaders do not require long roadmaps or huge backlogs. They determine what is most valuable right now to the ideal customers.

That's a huge problem because everything is uncertain, especially at the start of a project. But that uncertainty can help a product leader make better decisions faster. Here are some questions agile product leaders can answer with short experiments:

- Do I know who the ideal customers are?
- Do I know what problems they need to solve?
- What is the first (and then next) deliverable to help all of us learn if we are solving the right problems for the right customers?

An agile product leader focuses on small deliverables so everyone can learn as fast as possible. Those small deliverables allow a team to finish something valuable, release it, and then assess the results of that value.

That's why agile product leaders have a bias for shorter feedback loops based on small experiments.

However, an agile team and an agile product leader can't create short feedback loops if everyone works separately. That separate working has a name: resource efficiency.

1.3. Resource Efficiency Creates an Anti-Agility Culture

In a more traditional approach, managers assign, review, and sometimes control, the work each person performs. There's a name for that: resource efficiency.

Resource efficiency thinking assumes that product development is closer to factory work than to innovation and learning. If you've ever been part of a team that divided features into tasks, and then assigned specific tasks to specific people, you might have been working in resource efficiency.

The idea behind resource efficiency is seductive: It's possible to divide all the work so the "team" can conquer it. At the end of all that division, the features (or worse, the entire product) will magically come together. That looks efficient, both to the team and to the managers.

Divide and conquer *can* work for very small, straightforward problems and projects. However, it does not work for projects that take more than a few weeks or require innovation.

When managers think in resource efficiency, they tend to think about predictions vs. reality. They tend to measure schedule and schedule variation; cost and cost variation; and the busy-ness of the people, what they call "resource allocation."

However, until the team sees a completed feature, all those predictions are just that—predictions. They have no basis in reality.

Worse, when everyone realizes they're late, the team stops managing their technical excellence. Instead, they take shortcuts to meet the schedule, but they create future problems. Those problems result in late and unplanned feedback loops.

When managers focus on resource efficiency, they create multitasking at all levels: individual, team, and project. In turn, that creates very long feedback loops, high WIP (Work in Progress), and slow delivery of value.

Team members might cooperate, but they rarely collaborate, often because they have individual goals and objectives that might not have anything to do with this project.

That's why agile managers create a culture of flow efficiency.

1.4. Flow Efficiency Creates an Agile Culture

Flow efficiency thinking allows a team to focus on the flow of work through their system as individuals and as a team. You might have heard the maxim, "Watch the work, not the people." That's thinking in flow efficiency terms. (See *This is Lean: Resolving the Efficiency Paradox* [MOA13] for more details.)

When team members focus on the flow of work, they tend to collaborate more. Instead of handing off work to each other, they work together, finishing a feature. Teams that use flow efficiency tend to finish work and maintain that work's technical excellence.

In addition, managers can focus on the flow of work through the project portfolio by assigning teams to projects, not trying to play Tetris by assigning people to different projects. That allows managers to change their idea of the unit of work from an individual to a team.

When managers focus on flow, they create a culture where agility can thrive.

But if managers remain focused on the individual, as in resource efficiency, agility dies. That's when we see fake agility, where the teams live in agile death marches.

Teams and managers can't just *think* in flow efficiency. Instead, they need to change the measures they use at all levels.

1.4.1. Measures Change in Flow Efficiency

Here's what teams and managers can use for flow efficiency measures:

- WIP, the current number of work items in progress.
- Throughput, the number of work items completed per unit of time.
- Cycle time, the time to release value, at minimum internally, as a trend.
- Aging, how long a piece of work has been in progress.

Teams can use these measures for features while managers can use precisely the same measures for decisions. Once managers start to measure their decision aging, they realize that they tend to slow the work of everyone else because of their lack of decisions. (See *Why Minimize Management Decision Time* [ROT20] for actual data I measured in organizations.)

No balance sheet uses these measures—but they should. When teams and managers don't minimize WIP, reduce unnecessary waste in their cycle time, and address old work, their throughput goes way down, often to effectively zero.

As you might imagine, there's a relationship between WIP, throughput, and cycle time. That's called Little's Law.

Work in Progress (WIP) = Cycle Time * Throughput

Figure 1. Little's Law

WIP is a function of cycle time multiplied by the throughput. (See *The Kanban Pocket Guide: What No One Has Told You About Kanban Could Kill You* [VSJ22] for more information and all the caveats that go with this equation.)

Here's how I use Little's Law: When a team or a manager takes "too long" to finish work or make a decision, I might use a value stream map to see where the work is stuck. Or, I'll ask questions such as, "Does the team have enough skills and capabilities to finish their work?"

Sometimes, I review the arrival rate of new work. If more work arrives than the team can complete, the WIP increases. I worked with one team that completed three stories every week, but more than three stories arrived every week. Their WIP and cycle time grew, even though their throughput remained the same.

Flow metrics can help everyone—regardless of their position— reason about the actual project and product progress. Everyone can see the flow, or lack thereof, of all the work.

However, these measures don't count in cost accounting.

1.4.2. Cost Accounting Reinforces Resource Efficiency

Cost accounting focuses on the incremental value of building inventory and the variance between the projections and the actuals.

That can work for manufacturing, where the cost of adding value at each step in the manufacturing process can contribute to the overall added value of the product.

Software product development is not manufacturing. Teams create successful software and hardware products by learning and delivering together. While product development uses words from construction, the words don't mean the same thing.

Cost accounting reinforces resource efficiency thinking, where everyone focuses on the individual. That's why many organizations where everyone is overloaded and crazy-busy, but no one can finish anything, that low throughput problem the flow metrics assess.

Every organization needs to use cost accounting to *report* their profit and loss, pay taxes, and all the other external accounting activities. However, the more managers use flow efficiency to *manage* the business, the more agility can thrive.

That means that the measures organizations use to *report* their business state have limited to no use for *managing* the projects.

That's a huge cultural challenge for real agility. Because it feels "inefficient" to maintain two sets of measures. Except, it's actually easy to measure the flow metrics for any project or management effort.

But that's not the only problem. Flow efficiency thinking changes everything: career ladders, performance reviews, and how internal money flows from and to cost centers. (Cost centers and shared services "teams" take resource efficiency thinking to an extreme—and are anti-agile.)

In my experience, flow efficiency thinking is the most challenging change for an agile culture. And only the managers can change the organizational culture to focus on flow efficiency.

It's no wonder that agility-in-name, fake agility has won.

However, you can take advantage of agility where you find it.

1.5. Design Your Work to Take Advantage of Agility

With the exception of a strict waterfall lifecycle, you and your team can use any other approach or combination of approaches to design your project's lifecycle. That design will allow you to take advantage of agility where you can.

You might not be literally "agile," but you can be more effective. Especially when you can recognize and avoid the fake agile ideas.

1.6. Recognize and Avoid Fake Agility

In general, fake agile cultures overemphasize time to finish and de-emphasize learning. That leads to unplanned and long feedback loops. Worse, this emphasis on time often means the team has no autonomy to experiment with their process or the product.

Here are some examples of fake agility:

- The team creates a backlog for a week or two, but a manager wants a project manager to create a Gantt chart for the entire project—including these next two weeks.
- The team assigns all the stories to individuals in the team planning session.

- The team uses relative estimation instead of cycle time. As a result, all of their predictions are wrong—and they don't know why. Then, since the team doesn't deliver what they estimated, management asks them to do twice as much the next time.

Another example of fake agility is "Scrum-But" or "Water-Scrum-Fall." In Scrum-But, someone plans for the team, not with the team. Or the team doesn't perform demos or retrospectives on a regular basis.

In Water-Scrum-Fall, someone creates a year's worth of roadmaps or backlog, the team is supposed to use Scrum to deliver, and then a different team releases or deploys.

In both of these cases, the team doesn't learn from feedback and integrate that feedback into their work. This can occur with any agile approach, but because Scrum is the most "used" approach, this occurs most often with Scrum.

Fake agility removes the ease, joy, and flow of work. Worse, fake agility does not manage the customers' needs or the project's risks.

Instead, you can assess all the needs and risks and then choose a lifecycle that will work for you. You can even combine aspects of each lifecycle.

And if you have a culture where you can't call it a "whatever" lifecycle, you can even call it "our agile approach."

But whatever your approach, you can create some ease and joy in your work. That's the promise of choosing or designing your own lifecycle.

1.7. Remember This About True Agility

True agility is a cultural change. It requires:

- A collaborative, not just cooperative, team with all the skills and capabilities that the team needs to deliver value.
- A plan for the delivery of something useful for now, and then an updated plan based on what the team learned from their work on that delivery.
- A focus on a small amount of work right now, even if they need to maintain an open mind about the later work, such as the evolving architecture or user experience.

Flow efficiency thinking enables an agile culture. Resource efficiency thinking destroys an agile culture.

Let's start by examining how culture influences risks and tradeoffs.

Chapter 2. How Culture Influences Risks and Tradeoffs

Culture influences all aspects of projects, products, and management. That includes the risks each organization can tolerate, and the tradeoffs they might choose.

Each lifecycle differs in the risks they optimize for and against.

2.1. Lifecycles Manage Risks

A lifecycle is an idealized model of how to organize a project's work. That's it. While George Box referred to statistical models, his aphorism is correct for project lifecycles, too:

> "All models are wrong, but some models are useful."

Each lifecycle—as a model—addresses specific risks. Since most projects have multiple risks at different times, teams can choose the elements of each model to decide when to address their project's risks.

There are three major kinds of risks:

- Project-based risks, where the team needs to learn what customers think they want, learn together to create a shared understanding of how the emerging product works, and learn from what they did to plan for the next bit of work.

- Product-based risks, where the organization decides which customers they want to attract and when with the various features and feature sets.
- Portfolio-based risks, where management decides to start, transform, or stop a project. Effective portfolio management supports leadership's more effective corporate strategy.

Lifecycles help the team deliver its work so the product leader and managers can manage their decisions.

Let's start with the typical project risks.

2.2. Assess Your Project's Risks

For many years, we heard about the "iron triangle." Sometimes, the triangle was "Scope, Quality, Cost." Sometimes, it was "Scope, Date, Cost." It was always three things out of a minimum of four possibilities.

In my decades of participating in and managing projects, I've never seen a triangle of risks in practice. Instead, I've seen a pyramid of interconnected risks, as in the following figure.

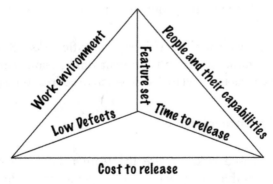

Figure 2. The Project Pyramid

Start on the inside of the pyramid, with the risks the project team can address directly. These risks often feel like pressure on the team. So how much pressure does your team feel to:

- Complete all the features (the requirements)
- With few or zero defects
- By the desired release date?

Then, there are the constraints management often attempts to impose on the project, on the outside of the pyramid:

- Cost to release (the costs to complete the project).
- People assigned to the project and the skills they have.
- Work environment, which includes where people are in the world and the project culture.

In my experience, management can and will change its mind about these supposed constraints, but that requires specific questions.

The more pressure the team feels, the less freedom the team has to manage its work. No lifecycle will work with an overconstrained project. That's why all projects must identify their necessary tradeoffs, so they can decide when they need feedback loops and decisions.

2.3. Project Tradeoffs Clarify Feedback Loops

Since every project has different risks, each project will require different feedback loops. That means each project needs to clarify its feedback loops before the project starts.

Before the project kickoff, I work to clarify the project's drivers, boundaries, and constraints, originally defined in *Manage It! Your*

Guide to Modern, Pragmatic Project Management [ROT07]. I use
this scenario:

"Assume you're three weeks from the desired release date. The
team hasn't finished all the features and won't in the next three
weeks. The testers continue to find problems, so the quality won't
be what we need. What do you want to do?"

I ask managers to rank the importance of each of the six sides of
the pyramid. Some sponsors want to claim each side is equally
important, but that is untrue. I remind them of the times the
sponsors added more people to the project or changed the team's
location, or invested in tooling as late project changes.

Only one side of the pyramid can *drive* the project. One or two
more sides might *bound* the project. But the remaining sides
are floats, and degrees of freedom that the project can use to
accomplish the work.

That's why I recommend project teams don't start to work until
they have a separate ranking for each side of the pyramid. That
information clarifies the necessary feedback loops.

When sponsors have to rank the tradeoffs, they might change their
minds about the outside of the pyramid. As a project manager, I
want management to see the reality of the project from the start.
When we discuss options to manage our reality, we can expose the
real constraints and break the fake constraints.

For example, if the sponsor says, "We're shipping on April 10.
Period. No excuses," then the release date is driving the project.
I often choose an incremental approach to make sure the project
completes as many features as possible in the time we have.

If the sponsor says, "We *must* have all these whiz-bang new
features," I can be sure we have plenty of technical risks. I'll use
an iterative approach to reduce the technical risks.

When sponsors say, "We must not break anything," I'll use an incremental approach with plenty of demos and tests. And to manage

the risks of regressions, I often ask for more testing capabilities through the architecture.

Regardless of lifecycle choice, a team can create a more agile culture when they collaborate to shorten their learning feedback loops, with each other and with the customers. Those shorter feedback loops allow the team to learn about the requirements and how the requirements should evolve as the customers start to use the product.

However, while *project* tradeoffs influence lifecycle choice, many teams also consider *product* risks to decide which lifecycle makes the most sense for this effort.

2.4. Assess Your Product's Innovation Risks

Most products require some innovation, but that innovation varies substantially during a product's lifetime. Consider the innovation continuum in the following figure.

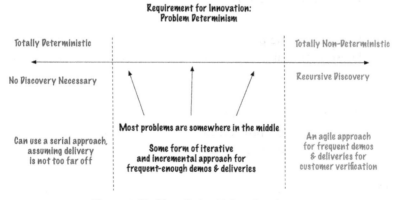

Figure 3. Problem Determinism Continuum

The innovative nature of the product also brings risks to the project.

The more innovative the product is (or the team believes it to be), the less the team can plan at any one time. That's because the team will need to iterate more frequently over the various features to obtain feedback and new decisions.

The more a team iterates over features, the more the team can review what they completed. They have the chance to replan future work every time they deliver some increment of value. Innovative products require more customer feedback and more frequent small planning.

The less innovative the product, the more the team can plan at one time. They don't have to worry as much about the changing nature of the product or what the customers expect. It's okay if their feedback loops are longer and there's more time between decisions.

These product risks are more subtle than the tradeoffs between features, defects, and time to release. However, product risks also affect any project's lifecycle choices.

2.5. Product Risks Can Drive Lifecycle Choice

Totally deterministic projects, those on the left of the continuum, can choose a serial approach. Those problems tend to be these kinds of work:

- Defect fixes, where the requirements won't change, or
- Small and short projects that take only one or two people for a maximum of four weeks.

The longer any project continues, the more likely someone will want something new or different. Even small, deterministic projects can morph into something closer to the middle of the continuum if they take more time than anyone expected.

For example, one of my clients completed a project to port an older product to new hardware. Originally, they thought they could use a serial approach. However, after the fifth week, they uncovered previously invisible problems in the old product that they did not want to port to the new product. They learned new information. They had a product squarely in the middle of the continuum.

Now, they needed more feedback loops and decisions. They still didn't have a totally innovative product, but they could not use a serial approach.

All the problems on the right of the continuum require fast feedback loops and frequent decisions to allow the project recursive discovery and delivery. That's where agile approaches shine. However, if your team can't create an agile culture, consider a combination lifecycle, where the team can spend some time iterating over features with sufficiently frequent deliveries.

But all those products in the middle of the innovation continuum? That's where teams can choose how and when to manage the risks. How can the product leader and the team slice and dice the feature sets into useful pieces of value? Which customers need which slices sooner or later? How often do the customers see the work?

That's why the product innovation risks require more subtle lifecycle choices—and probably, more combinations of lifecycles in the same project.

The more innovation your product requires, the more feedback loops and decision points your project needs.

Your Organization's Culture Might Reflect Its Products

Years ago, I worked with an insurance company. By nature— because of the products they sold—they were risk averse. Even though they continued to lose market share, they had a terrible time using agile ideas because they were so focused on the statistical modeling of risk.

Organizations attract people who want to work on the organization's products. That might reinforce a culture that does not appear to invite agility. However, it's possible to explain the benefits and the risks in ways that will encourage people to reconsider their risk exposure.

Once they realized they could purposefully iterate on prototypes, and then move to incremental deliveries, they did. That allowed them to innovate on their next generation of products.

When product leaders and teams choose which features to expose and when, they can create the necessary project feedback loops and decision points. Those decisions allow the team to gather project and product feedback.

In turn, all that feedback can support how the team organizes the next part of the project. That's how teams can use product risks to help manage project risks.

2.6. Product Feedback Loops Reduce Risks

The most common product risks revolve around identifying the ideal (buying) customer who has problems that this product solves. The next set of risks is the timing: when the team needs to release which features for these ideal customers.

The more often the team experiments and delivers something useful, the faster the product leader can manage those risks.

That means that as the teams iterate over the requirements and deliver something useful, a product leader needs to be able to change the list of features and the order in which the team delivers those features.

That means the project team needs to deliver increments of value to verify the product solves the customers' problems. As the product leader and the team learn together, the product leader might change the order and type of deliverables as everyone learns what customers need.

An agile culture supports frequent customer identification and feedback.

Finally, organization-based risks, such as project portfolio management can affect a team's lifecycle choice.

2.7. Portfolio-Based Risks Can Drive Lifecycle Choice

Imagine a startup, where they're searching for the right combination of features for the right customers, so they can grow fast. These organizations need the project(s) to deliver something fast, and frequently.

Or, imagine a large organization that realizes its market is totally changing and they need to cancel projects and decide where to place their bets.

Or, imagine an established innovative organization whose current customers have requested a variety of features. After reviewing those requests, the leaders realize all those requests can create a new product that requires several teams to deliver. The leaders decide to create a program, to deliver that one business objective.

The organization's leaders can't take advantage of these opportunities unless each team learns as the team proceeds. That learning allows the team to inform management of the product's progress. Once management understands the product's progress, management can make good decisions.

The project portfolio can affect any team's choice for its lifecycle.

2.8. Agile Strategy Risks

Managers need the ability to reconsider the organization's strategy. Since the project portfolio reflects the organization's strategy, managers want to be able to start, transform, or stop a given project. Most managers realize they might need a week or two to start, transform, or stop—but most managers I know don't want to wait more than a week or two before they make a decision.

But culture can eclipse any of the needs and risks. That's because culture creates a system of work.

2.9. Culture Creates the Overall System of Work

Edgar Schein in *Organizational Culture and Leadership* [SCH10] says that our artifacts, values, and assumptions define our culture. Consider these three questions as a way to assess your culture:

- How do we treat each other?
- What can we discuss?
- What do we reward?

There is no wrong or right culture, but agile approaches work best when team members treat each other with respect and collaborate to finish work. Agile approaches also work well when managers avoid rewarding heroics and firefighting, and instead, reward steady team-based completion.

On the other hand, a serial lifecycle tends to reinforce a command and control approach to the work, because that culture prizes predictability, a need for order, and the quest for stability. (Serial lifecycles only *look* predictable. They have the most unplanned feedback loops.)

In emergencies, we might need a command and control leader who can lead us to a safe place. However, most of the time, teams don't need controlling leadership.

That's why agile approaches require a cultural change. Not just to manage the various risks and meet everyone's needs, but because teams can manage their work themselves. Including selecting a lifecycle that will meet everyone's needs.

The biggest way to meet everyone's needs is to focus on learning during the project.

2.10. Project Learning Helps Manage Risks

Excluding the serial approaches, each lifecycle encourages some form of learning as the project progresses.

The project and product risks create two learning loops: in the project and for the product.

1. *Project* feedback loops allow the people to incorporate learning to decide how to work next.
2. *Product* feedback loops allow people to make decisions about what to do next, both for this product and for the overall project portfolio.

In addition, the portfolio risks might change the product decisions— which might prompt the team to change how they work.

The more your lifecycle focuses on learning throughout the project, the more the team can adapt to these changing needs.

All lifecycles include learning—even if that learning arrives late in the project. The earlier the learning, the more likely the project and the product will succeed.

When a project team learns together, they can better see and manage the project and product risks. Add in the fact that any product innovation—even the middle of the innovation continuum—requires learning, here's a question I recommend you ask:

How can my project team learn faster and better?

The single most important tip I can offer is to create a single cross-functional team that will:

- Work on all parts of the project, from analysis to release, together,
- starting on the first day,
- with no other interrupting work,
- until the last day, whether that last day is a cancellation or a release.

No visitors to the team. No single-function people or teams who might start and leave the effort before completion. No waiting for other people that the project needs before they can complete the work. And definitely, no other additional work.

Instead, create one cross-functional team that owns the effort and can learn together. When the team can assess, experiment, and solve problems together, they can create a valuable outcome—the product.

No project can avoid learning. If your project does not require learning, it doesn't have risks, which means it's closer to a checklist than a project.

If someone insists you organize a project in a way that does not include learning or decision points, the project will fail. That's a huge risk.

2.11. Remember This About Culture, Risks, and Tradeoffs

Your current culture, risks, and tradeoffs will define what you can do to create a more agile culture that focuses on flow efficiency, short feedback loops, and integrating customer feedback into your products.

1. Start with your risks by assessing your project's drivers, constraints, and floats to see what's driving and bounding your project. (If your project is part of a program, each project might have its own driver. Some projects will need to experiment more and some projects might need to deliver value faster.)
2. Consider how often your project needs feedback from your customer or other stakeholders and partners.
3. Decide when you want information from what your team finished to inform the next part of your project.
4. If your product requires innovation, the team can learn faster with shorter feedback loops. Those feedback loops will help you replan more often, to innovate faster.
5. The more often your managers want to change the project portfolio, the more your project will need faster feedback loops and decision points.

Each lifecycle optimizes for different duration feedback loops and deliveries. Let's start at the beginning with a serial lifecycle and why many managers appear to like the serial lifecycle so much.

Chapter 3. Serial Lifecycles

Serial lifecycles exist when the project completes each step of the project *in order* before continuing to the next step. Waterfall, phase gate, or stage gate are all examples of serial approaches.

Serial lifecycles manage very few of the project, product, or portfolio risks outlined in the previous chapter. But these lifecycles *look* logical, as if they should manage those risks.

3.1. Serial Lifecycles Look Logical

Many serial lifecycles look something like the next figure.

Requirements	Analysis	Design	Code	Integration	Test	Release

Figure 4. Serial Lifecycle

Here's how the serial lifecycle is supposed to work:

1. The people responsible for requirements attempt to define "all" the requirements first, often in a document. Often, some group of people sign off on the requirements.
2. Next, some functional group does "all" the analysis, often in a document. (Often, this is where an architect defines the product architecture.) Many organizations institute a signoff here, too.
3. Then, some functional group does "all" the detailed design, often in many documents. Again, with design reviews, people sign off on the design.

4. Then, the coders code from the detailed design. They often try to finish "all" the code. And they might use code reviews and other people sign off on the code.
5. Finally, the testers either use their previously created tests (often in documents) or now create tests and test "all" the code.
6. The product is ready for delivery.

These steps look logical. And because the steps are in order, we can use words such as "phase" or "stage" to define each step.

Serial lifecycles are an idealized approach to product development—and they rarely work. Worse, they reinforce resource efficiency.

That work separation creates many problems with serial lifecycles.

While the signoffs appear to be decision points, people can only sign off based on documents, not visible *product* progress. There are no demos or other visible ways to see the progress.

A true serial lifecycle does not show any product until the testing phase. That means the decision points are based on *project* measures which rarely have anything to do with the product. Those measures tend to be schedule or cost variance.

But back in Section 2.1: Lifecycles Manage Risks on page 13, I said that date and schedule risks are part of the tradeoffs projects can make. So measuring any variance doesn't help, unless you *also* measure the product progress.

Serial lifecycles have many problems.

3.2. Visualize Problems with Serial Lifecycles

Serial lifecycles can succeed for a small project of a few people up to three or four weeks in duration. But serial lifecycles fail when the effort requires more people or more time. That's because someone will learn something late—a big risk. See Section 2.10: Project Learning Helps Manage Risks on page 23.

Serial lifecycles have these assumptions:

- The project will succeed if each *function* finishes its work before starting another function. Often, that means a functional person or group works on the project alone, not a cross-functional team of people who learn together.
- And that the end of a phase means some people can hand off their work to the next people in line and *never* have to return to this project again in a future phase.
- That the project does not have to do risk management in case something happens with any of the phases. For years, people told me a serial lifecycle would work if they could "just" get the requirements right. But that would mean we could perfectly predict the requirements. Then, we needed to get the architecture "right." Same thing for detailed design.

I've never seen any of these assumptions hold true in a successful project. All of those assumptions are anti-learning.

Instead, I saw many realities of serial lifecycles, such as:

- The requirements took too long to finish
- No phase ever met "freeze" or "complete" before release.
- The project had plenty of unplanned feedback loops.

Let's take each of these in order.

3.2.1. Requirements Takes "Too Long"

Years ago, a project manager, Jim, explained his problem. "Our requirements phase takes way too long. As a result, we often shortchange the testing. But if we do that, we have more problems in the next release. What do I do?"

Jim described the problem in the next figure, where requirements take "too long."

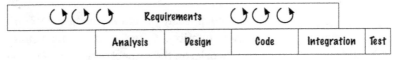

Figure 5. Requirements Take Too Long

Jim described this project as the "never-ending hell of the require-ments phase." Requirements Hell exists—and still exists today, even in so-called agile projects. (For more information, see *Manage It! Your Guide to Modern, Pragmatic Project Management* [ROT07].)

Jim's organization had these problems:

- Because they had too few product managers, they used intermittent planning for the projects, not continual planning. So the product manager assigned to this project had to drop everything and plan for the next project. That was how they started the planning for this project.
- But as the product manager discovered more information, the product manager added more requirements. Worse, this company used a form of "MoSCoW" prioritization, the Must, Should, Could, Walk-the-Dog-first prioritization, not a strict ranking. (Most people call the W ranking "Would," but Jim's organization realized they would never get to the Would requirements.)
- The longer the requirements phase, the more the require-ments changed and the more the prioritization changed.

But when projects use a serial lifecycle, any phase might not end.

Sometimes, managers want to predict the next phase or the end of the project based on when the previous phase "completes" or "freezes." But the project might never freeze or complete anything until the final release.

3.2.2. Freeze or Complete Never Occurs

In this next problem, the project manager tries to create a schedule with freezes. (I could have written "Complete" for these milestones, but I saw the word "Freeze" more often.)

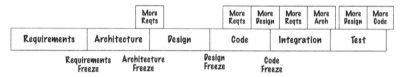

Figure 6. Freezes are Slush

Mary, a project manager, tried to create a Gantt chart, complete with freezes. However, as the architects completed the architecture phase, they created feedback loops to the requirements phase. The same thing occurred in the Code, Integration, and Test phases.

Her manager asked when she expected the requirements phase to end. She said, "When we ship. That's when all the phases will end."

Mary could not predict the end of the project. Instead, she continued to negotiate the project-level tradeoffs from Section 2.3: Project Tradeoffs Clarify Feedback Loops on page 15.

Mary's boss told her to "plan the work and work the plan." Because they had to ship the product in four months, they were somewhat able to do so. Although, they did not ship most of the requirements they had defined.

Longer duration serial lifecycle projects often have even more feedback loops that overwhelm any forward progress as in the next problem of unplanned feedback loops.

3.2.3. Unplanned Feedback Loops Create Unpredictability

Other lifecycles plan for feedback loops. But a serial lifecycle does not. When the project uses a serial approach, the project can encounter many unplanned feedback loops, as in the next figure.

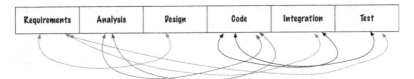

| Requirements | Analysis | Design | Code | Integration | Test |

Figure 7. Many Unplanned Feedback Loops

The longer the project takes, the more unplanned feedback loops the project will have. That's because the people on the project don't plan *for* change. Worse, the more likely the project will become a death march, or realize one of those unplanned feedback loops becomes the project Kiss of Death.

Years ago, I consulted on a project where senior management insisted on a waterfall approach for an eighteen-month project. When I arrived, they were six months in and had no idea when they could finish anything—not the requirements, the analysis, or the detailed design. Their feedback loops were out of control.

They wanted me to tell them precisely *when* the project would complete each phase.

I told them no one could answer that question. They had ways to manage the risks, but I certainly couldn't tell them when any phase would end because there was no way to manage the various feedback loops. (I suggested they start pruning their current requirements, so they could finish and release *something* useful.)

The more innovation risks, the less likely a team can get anything (requirements, analysis, design, tests, whatever) right the first time. Projects need feedback loops to assess how right the product is now and what to do in the future.

The shorter the feedback loop, the easier it is for a team to plan *for* change. Short feedback loops enable teams to reduce their WIP, make smaller changes, use technical excellence, and refactor regularly.

There are plenty more possible problems with a serial lifecycle. However, in my experience, the worst problem is that the serial lifecycle focuses on the individual people doing "their" jobs, not on the product itself.

3.3. Serial Lifecycles Fake a Focus on the Work

One of the reasons for the unanticipated feedback loops is the serial lifecycles focus on the current phase or function, not the project or product team. Too often, that phase requires one group of people who then hand off the work to the next functional group.

That *looks* like flow efficiency thinking, but it's not. This is a focus on an individual or an individual function, not a collaborative cross-functional team. (See Section 1.3: Resource Efficiency Creates an Anti-Agility Culture on page 5.)

Worse, a serial lifecycle creates much WIP, because the project attempts to address *all* the requirements, architecture, design, etc. before the team creates any usable or visible piece of the product. That's why a serial lifecycle is anti-agile—it's focused on resource efficiency, not flow efficiency.

If you must use a serial lifecycle, create a cross-functional team that will work together on the project, from the start to the finish.

Since successful product development requires a cross-functional team that can learn together, successful projects focus on the speed of the entire team, that idea of flow efficiency.

But it doesn't matter if you plan for feedback or not—every project will need feedback at some point. And every project needs decision points to decide how to proceed.

3.4. Successful Projects Incorporate Feedback

Why do organizations still use a waterfall or other serial lifecycle? First, the simplicity of the project *looks* like the serial lifecycle should work. But I suspect the reality is even simpler. People got impatient reading Winston Royce's original paper, *Managing the Development of Large Software Systems* from 1987 [ROY87] and never got past the first page.

On the first page of the paper, Royce shows the start of a serial lifecycle. Then on page two, he shows a waterfall. Directly underneath that picture, he says, "I believe in this concept, but the implementation described above is risky and invites failure."

Just two pages later, he starts to describe the various feedback loops. The rest of the paper is full of possible feedback loops.

Royce, the so-called "father" of a waterfall lifecycle, thought a waterfall approach was too risky. He wanted to see feedback loops.

However, I have seen managers use phases or gates as a way to cancel projects.

3.5. Serial Lifecycles Can Allow Early Cancellation

Back in the 1970s and 1980s, some managers used the information after each phase to choose when to cancel projects. That's where the idea of the "stage gate" or "phase gate" was born. The manager could assess the progress at the end of each stage or phase and decide whether to cancel the project.

This cancellation approach works well if the entire cross-functional team works together on each phase as in the next figure.

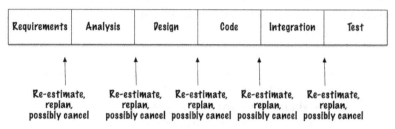

Figure 8. Serial Lifecyle with the Option to Cancel

Here's how the cancellation worked:

- The team assessed the information from the previous phase, including how long it took them to finish that work, compared to their estimate.
- Based on that information they could then re-estimate how much more work they had. (Note: This is a feedback loop.)
- With that information, they could replan or cancel the project.

When project teams used previous information to inform their next planning, they were as agile as they could have been at the time, given that they had no input from their customers.

However, being able to cancel the project early is the only benefit I see to serial lifecycles for projects longer than a few weeks or that require more than a couple of people. Instead, I see many problems with serial lifecycles.

3.6. Serial Lifecycles Create Project-Based Risks

Serial lifecycles create at least two levels of problems: project-based risks, and organization-based problems. Let's start with the project-based risks. These include:

- Strong tendency to implement across the architecture, not through the architecture. That's a risk because no one has any insight into real product progress. The first time the team sees a feature is when the testers start.
- Substantial WIP, including each phase's documentation.
- Lack of team collaboration and learning due to the focus on *one* skill set at a time.

Let's start with implementation across the architecture and why that's a problem.

3.6.1. Implement Across the Architecture, Not Through

The more functional experts hand off "their" work to the next function, the more unplanned feedback loops occur. I already said that makes it impossible to freeze or complete phases. (See Section 3.2.2: Freeze or Complete Never Occurs on page 31.) Worse, those functional experts *tend* to work across the architecture, not through it, as in the next image.

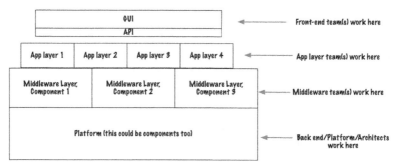

Figure 9. Implement Across the Architecture

Because these experts tend to work alone, no one has any real insight into project progress until the testers start. Testing exposes the actual feature progress. If the team uses Concurrent Engineering, they might not fall into this trap.

Concurrent Engineering Refers to the Team

Back in the 1990s, people realized projects needed whole teams, which led to the term "Concurrent Engineering." Instead of enforcing when certain people worked on which phase of the project, the entire team worked together, from the start, concurrently.

Worse, when people work across the architecture, they don't realize when they have incomplete work, whether that is architecture, code, or tests. The team cannot maintain its technical excellence because they do not see any part of a finished product.

The more the project works across the architecture, the more WIP the project has.

3.6.2. High WIP (Work In Progress)

Because the documentation is supposed to explain how the product will work, many serial projects realize they have reams and reams of documentation. That creates two kinds of WIP:

- Documentation WIP, where the documents multiply, and change, often too fast for everyone on the project to stay current.
- Feature WIP, because each phase's documentation requires the team to address every single feature.

As an example, imagine one team member starts the detailed design for a specific feature. But the current architecture does not support that design. That team member must take time to discuss the architectural needs with the architect who designed the original architecture. However, because the architect thought they were done, they are now working on other products.

The team member doing the design has to wait for the architect. Since the culture focuses on resource efficiency and busy-ness, the team member starts to design another feature. The team member increases their personal and team WIP by one.

That's not the only increase in WIP. When the architect stops their current work to handle this interrupt, the architect increases their WIP by one. So one interruption on one project can cause higher WIP on a different project.

Imagine that circumstance applying to each person on the team for each requirement. Everyone is busy, but no one can finish anything. That's an example of Figure 1: Little's Law on page 8 at work.

While the team can determine the necessary changes, those changes often take a long time.

But high WIP and low throughput also have other costs. The older an item is, the less anyone remembers the details about the item. And the more likely the person who started that item is no longer with the project, or even the organization.

High WIP, just like multitasking, can kill project momentum. The project can also see a lack of momentum when the project people work alone, not as a collaborative team.

3.6.3. Lack of Teamwork

Serial lifecycles reinforce the idea of resource efficiency, where one person can finish their work alone. However, I already said that product development requires the team to learn. And the faster the team can learn together, the faster they can complete the project.

The more managers want to slice and dice people's time, to make sure people are maximally busy, the longer the project takes. That's because working in flow efficiency, where a team of people takes responsibility for the project and its outcomes is the fastest way to finish a project.

The more management focuses on the *people* and not the *work*, the less teamwork the project has. Less teamwork creates slower learning and longer release times—exactly what managers do not want.

This leads us to organization-based problems.

3.7. Serial Lifecycles Create Organization-Based Problems

While there are more problems, these are the major organization-wide problems with a serial lifecycle:

- The time delays and therefore costs of a serial lifecycle are invisible to management.
- Instead of seeing product-based outcomes, a serial lifecycle emphasizes outputs, such as documents.
- Significant multitasking because individual people can't progress on *their* work. (These people often need the rest of the team.) Instead, they start another piece of work. And too often people start another project, regardless of a late piece of feedback on one project.
- That multitasking challenges any real portfolio management.

Most of this is invisible to management and to the people on the project.

3.7.1. Invisible Time Delays and Costs

Every time I see a serial lifecycle project, I see people working hard. They often work overtime to finish their work so they can hand that work off to the next person or team.

And too often, the people on the initial task have questions for other people. But the people with the answers are not available.

That lack of availability adds to the cycle time of all the work. Aside from late feedback loops, the other people's lack of availability creates late projects.

Worse, the late feedback loops make it even more difficult to finish the coding and testing, even with "complete" documentation. There is no such thing as "complete" documentation. Even if there was such a thing, documentation, by itself, is rarely sufficient for product outcomes. That's because documentation does not create team-based learning.

Outputs, such as documentation, can support product development. However, outputs alone, are not sufficient.

3.7.2. Belief that Outputs are Sufficient for Product Outcomes

In a serial approach, many people—managers and team members—believe that "complete" documentation will make it easier to finish the coding and test the product. Too often, these people believe that after "complete" documentation, product development is a SMOP (Simple Matter of Programming).

However, programming—the actual typing—is the least time-consuming step in product development. Long ago, I spent three weeks designing and coding a particularly complex piece of a product. We had a hard disk crash and the code was all gone. But I was able to recreate the program in about six hours—because I had already learned what the product needed to do.

That's the same issue in any project. The programming of the code or the tests takes very little time. The team's understanding and learning—that's what takes time.

Teams arrive at shared understanding—those unintentional or unplanned feedback loops—as they build the outcomes, the product itself.

Is there a time to create documentation? If your product requires documentation, consider these options from *Manage It!* [ROT07]:

- Start with images of candidate architectures, and refine those images as the team prototypes and completes features.
- Add detailed documentation as the team completes features, especially if your product needs to offer user-based guides.
- Decide where insufficient documentation is a risk and plan to manage that risk.

Each of these options will help the team learn together, which will reduce the project's risks.

But, if people are not available to learn together, everyone starts to multitask.

3.7.3. Significant Multitasking

Imagine this scenario: you arrive at work Monday morning to work on an exciting product. The team already had the kickoff meeting and you want to finish your feature this week.

But, you need answers from someone else. That person won't be available for at least a few hours. So you start the next feature. Why would you start a new feature? Because your managers prize busy-ness over completion.

Don't blame the managers. Cost accounting *discourages* team-work. (That's one reason agile approaches require a cultural change.)

But the more other people aren't available, the more likely everyone is to start new work. And not just new work on this project, but possibly new projects.

The more multitasking one person has, the higher the overall WIP and the lower the teamwork, precisely the conditions that work *against* an early-as-possible release.

In addition, rampant multitasking makes it impossible for managers to manage the project portfolio.

3.7.4. Inability to Perform Adequate Portfolio Management

The more multitasking, the less likely managers feel they can stop or cancel projects. That's because all the projects are stuck, waiting to expose their progress on various milestones.

In reality, managers can stop working on many projects and assign teams of people to projects. For more information, see *Manage Your Project Portfolio: Increase Your Capacity and Finish More Projects, 2nd ed* [ROT16B].

So with all the problems of a serial lifecycle, why do managers like them so much?

3.8. Why Some Managers Like a Serial Approach

Some managers still tell me they long for the days of the waterfall or phase gate. They say things like, "I could understand the project." Or, "They worked when I was an engineer." Worse, the manager says, "I can predict with a phase gate."

These managers are partially right.

A serial lifecycle hides all the necessary feedback loops in a simple visualization or a Gantt chart. Because the visualization hides these feedback loops, managers think they can understand the work. (In reality, if the managers reviewed PERT charts instead of a Gantt, they would see the decision points.)

And, sometimes, a serial approach does work. Back when these managers worked as engineers, the problems were simpler and the projects were shorter—two conditions that make it possible for a serial lifecycle to succeed. However, given how much the world has changed since then, I find it difficult to believe any innovative product development can use a serial lifecycle now.

But the manager's ability to predict?

That's a false sense of prediction. The various phases and freezes and milestones hide all the learning and the feedback loops. Worse, when someone creates a Gantt chart from these milestones, they create a single-point estimate.

Estimations and predictions are guesses, not empirical data. Guesses tend to be wrong. And single-point estimates are almost always wrong.

Back in the early days of software development, serial lifecycles helped savvy managers manage costs when they canceled the project. "If we spent this much so far, and we've only done half the requirements (or half the design or coding), can we afford to do the rest of the work?" That was especially true when release costs were very high.

But now, software-only products have very low release costs. Even if your product requires integration with hardware or firmware, you might have higher external release costs. But, almost all projects can show internal demos, if not release the product as the project proceeds.

However, there are plenty of culture challenges with a serial lifecycle.

3.9. Culture Challenges with a Serial Lifecycle

Because serial lifecycles reinforce planning without experimentation and prediction without feedback, they tend to create a culture of control, specifically of people outside the team controlling the people inside the team. Serial lifecycles tend to reinforce resource efficiency thinking.

These challenges exist in many serial lifecycle projects:

- Little to no focus on the flow of the work, and a lot of focus on how busy each person is. That leads to a title-based leader, such as a project manager, who assigns work to people, often with an expected completion date. Too often, that work is not an outcome that offers anyone value, such as a full story or requirement, but a task. When leaders focus on resource efficiency, they create multitasking and reduce everyone's learning. Too few serial projects have a collaborative team because they work as individuals with little interaction.

- Senior leaders tend to do a lot of up-front work. (The term for this is "Big Design Up Front," but can refer to anything without customer-based feedback.) Product managers try to specify all the requirements, often, including the user interface. Architects try to specify the design before the team even sees the requirements. That shortcuts the team's ability to learn from internal or customer-based experiments. Many of the unplanned feedback loops occur because all projects require some learning.
- Someone estimates for the team. Instead of explaining the outcomes and estimating small pieces of work, the team is supposed to estimate the entire project. That means that either the team interrupts what it's doing now, causing multitasking, or someone estimates on behalf of the team. While I don't know how far off someone else's estimate will be, I can guarantee that estimate is wrong.
- Managers have to wait for quarters and years to evaluate the product to manage the project portfolio and the corporate strategy. That leads to yearly funding, which leads to much more management dysfunction. In addition, the longer it takes managers to re-evaluate the project portfolio, the more likely they are to ask for estimates of all the work. Those estimates create multitasking.

Control cultures are anti-agile. If your product requires innovation, or your managers need to cancel projects more often than when a team can complete a product, avoid a serial lifecycle.

3.10. Tips to Make a Serial Lifecycle Work for You

If your management wants your project to use a serial lifecycle, here are some ideas to make it work better:

1. Create several smaller projects, and incrementally release them. So instead of one large release, you'd have Release 1, then 1.1, then 1.2, and so on. That will reduce each releases's WIP.
2. Create a cross-functional team that stays with the project from start to end. That increases the team's learning and can reduce the team's cycle time.
3. Use probabilistic estimation and update it at the end of each phase. This will help everyone realize that any previous estimate is unreliable, and can't be reliable until the product is in testing.

I've had good results limiting the up-front requirements, architecture, and design phases and then moving to an incremental lifecycle to absorb the feedback loops. Once people got to see the product as the team built it, they cared less about the lifecycle and much more about the product.

3.11. Remember This About Serial Lifecycles

Serial lifecycles look logical and orderly. However, the reality is that because they have unplanned feedback and no specific milestone for updated decisions, they rarely work.

If your organization wants to use a serial lifecycle, consider these ways to manage your project's risks:

1. Make sure your project has a cross-functional team where everyone works 100% on this project and only this project.
2. Consider measuring the WIP and the delays of working this way. (See Section 1.4.1: Measures Change in Flow Efficiency on page 7). If nothing else, a value stream map might encourage people to collaborate more.

3. Consider creating internal releases every few weeks. That might reduce the organization's reliance on documentation instead of product development.
4. If your project will last longer than six months or so, consider splitting that project into releases that last a maximum of six months.

If your managers insist they need estimates, have them read *Manage Your Project Portfolio: Increase Your Capacity and Finish More Projects, 2nd ed* [ROT16B]. Managers make much better decisions when they use value instead of estimation to decide on the project portfolio.

All projects can incorporate feedback during the project, to see what the project has accomplished and use that to inform the next bit of planning and releasing.

And that's the point of the next chapter, a discussion of iterative lifecycles to encourage feedback and manage risks.

Chapter 4. Iterative Lifecycles

Since a serial lifecycle proves no one can plan everything "right" at the start, projects can plan to iterate, especially based on customer feedback.

That's what the iterative lifecycles do. They optimize for technical risk because they focus on customer collaboration with frequent customer feedback.

Barry Boehm proposed the first iterative lifecycle in 1988, as a spiral model, integrating customer feedback.

4.1. Spiral Model Focuses on Customer Feedback

In 1988, Barry Boehm suggested a "spiral" model of software development. Boehm suggested a spiral of successive prototype development, with a final finishing step. Each step depended on customer input.

His paper, *A Spiral Model of Software Development and Enhancement* [BOE86] not only referred to Royce's proposal for feedback loops, but also for Royce's proposal for iterative development. (The idea of "Build it twice.")

Boehm suggested that each movement around the spiral should address the objective for this part of the product, any alternatives for implementation, and the constraints.

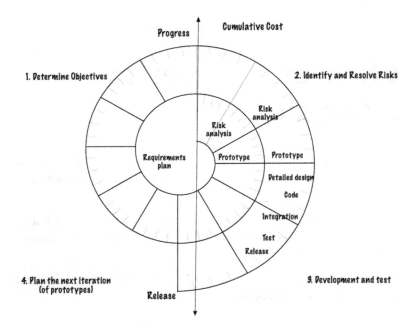

Figure 10. Boehm's Spiral Model

The project first starts with objectives, which leads to a requirements plan. Then, with some requirements, the team does risk analysis and works with customers to find win-win solutions.

The team resolves risks with each prototype. In my experience, the third step of Development and Test was only for throw-away prototypes and only for one feature set or feature at a time. Then, the team and the customers would plan for the next iteration of prototypes.

The team and the customers worked their way around the spiral as long as they needed to. The result of these prototypes was a detailed design, which the team could use to create their final code. Then, they could integrate all the code, test it, and release it.

However, many managers had trouble visualizing the *project* if it was in a spiral. It certainly wasn't possible to create a Gantt or a

PERT chart to show the project. So I used the following figure to show my managers what I meant by an iterative lifecycle.

Require-ments	Prototype: Analysis, design, code. Check with customer. Replan based on feedback	Prototype: Analysis, design, code. Check with customer. Replan based on feedback	Prototype: Analysis, design, code. Check with customer. Replan based on feedback	... As many prototypes as necessary	Finish the prototypes: Complete the development work	Integration	Test

Each prototype can be a different duration.
Remaining boxes not to scale with time.

Figure 11. My Experiences with Spiral Lifecycles

I suspect that Boehm did not specifically restrict the requirements gathering and definition time, but I did. That helped the product manager and the customers decide what to work on now and what to work on later.

Then, each prototype had its own time. If the team and the customers thought the prototyping took "too long," the customer helped clarify what to postpone and what to continue.

However, in my experience, the final finishing did not create detailed design documents. And, the projects I worked on didn't always throw away every prototype. However, because iterative projects ask for customer feedback all along, many iterative projects delivered a satisfactory product.

There's an alternative to a spiral model, and that's an Evolutionary Prototyping Lifecycle.

4.2. Evolutionary Prototyping Focuses on the Product

I only used an evolutionary prototyping lifecycle once. It was a custom four-person project for a Very Important Customer. The customer agreed to work with us, so we could speed up our work.

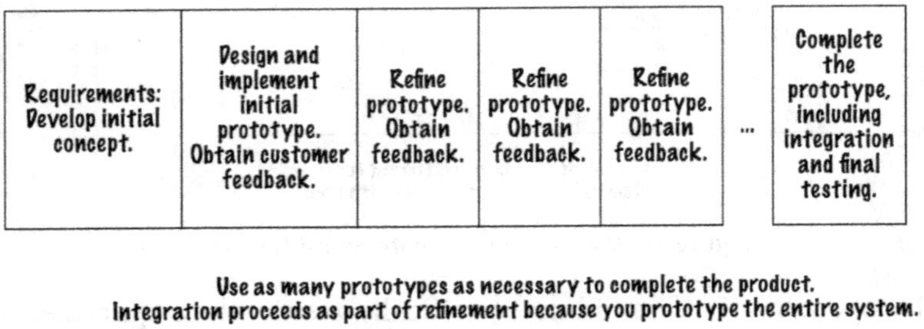

Requirements: Develop initial concept.	Design and implement initial prototype. Obtain customer feedback.	Refine prototype. Obtain feedback.	Refine prototype. Obtain feedback.	Refine prototype. Obtain feedback.	...	Complete the prototype, including integration and final testing.

Use as many prototypes as necessary to complete the product.
Integration proceeds as part of refinement because you prototype the entire system.

Figure 12. Evolutionary Prototyping

In the project I worked on, we used a form of "successive refinement." The team took one feature or a small feature set, prototyped it, and showed it to the customer. Then, once the customer approved, we built the next feature on top of that prototype.

I'm not sure what we were *supposed* to do, but we finished all the code as the customer approved it. We only threw away prototypes when the customer didn't like what we had done. If the customer liked the prototype, we hardened the code if necessary.

In addition to the Spiral model and Evolutionary prototyping, any of the "Unified" processes are primarily iterative lifecycles.

4.3. Unified Processes Integrate Phases with Some Deliveries

In the 1990s, the Rational Software Corporation started developing its Rational Unified Process, RUP. IBM later bought that company and retained the name.

The four phases in RUP are:

- Inception, where the cross-functional team develops use cases to iterate through the requirements and business modeling.
- Elaboration, where the team mostly completes their use cases, fleshes out the architecture, and starts initial development and testing.
- Construction, where the team completes the bulk of the development and testing.
- Deployment where the team starts and finishes deployment.

RUP has evolved since the early 2000s, now turning into SAFe, but many teams who use it also use these practices:

- Use of timeboxes, often called release trains, to deliver what the teams completed since the previous release. Pioneered by Cisco and Sun in the 1980s, the train always left on the same (relative) day of the month or quarter. Teams merged their finished work into the product version for the next train. See *Manage It! Your Guide to Modern, Pragmatic Project Management* [ROT07] for more information. In the UP projects I saw, teams did not start any trains until after significant development and testing.
- Frequent, if not continuous integration, to finish the next batch of work.
- Focus on higher risk and possibly higher value features, via use cases.

My UP experience is quite limited. Over my consulting career, I have worked with about twenty supposedly RUP projects. About half of them did not iterate over the requirements and, because of the phases, became serial lifecycle projects.

The other half stopped iterating with feedback over requirements and became incremental projects, often with release trains. I'll discuss my release train experience in the next chapter.

The point of the four phases is to purposefully iterate over the requirements using feedback, to improve/change the business model, architecture, and overall design. I never saw that. But, as I said, I have very little experience with any of the UPs.

All the iterative approaches, because they do not include few or infrequent deliveries, create challenges for teams and projects.

4.4. Challenges for Iterative-Only Lifecycles

If the project team works continually with the customer, iterative lifecycles can work. However, because these lifecycles only have one delivery at the end, these lifecycles run the risk of requirements changes if the project continues for too long.

Worse, sometimes these iterative-only lifecycles experience a project Kiss of Death if they experience late feedback loops.

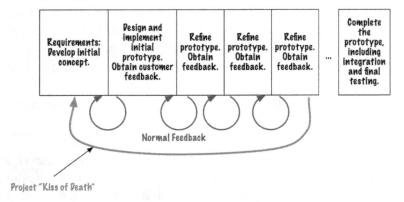

Figure 13. Late Iterative Lifecycle Feedback Loops

The team and the customer expect some feedback on earlier prototypes. That was the point of iterating through the prototypes.

But the Kiss of Death occurs when the team and the customer realize very late in the project that they need to return to the requirements. Everything needs to change.

Here are their choices:

1. Cancel the project now. That's a lot of sunk cost, so most managers don't want to do that.
2. Finish the work to release the product as is.
3. Bite the bullet and return to the requirements and see what else the team needs to do.

In my experience, very few managers like any of these choices.

However, the iterative lifecycles offer more agility in replanning because of customer feedback.

4.5. Opportunities for Agility

Iterative lifecycles expect frequent feedback and frequent decisions because the cross-functional team and the customer work together.

- They can replan when and what the customer wants in the next prototype.
- Once the team completes a few prototypes, the team might have insight into more accurate estimates for the next piece of work.
- The team's progress is visible, so management and the customer can decide whether to continue investing in the project.

If teams use short feedback loops, the product leader and the team can plan *for* change. When teams plan for change, they tend to plan to refactor more often. That frequent refactoring allows the team to more easily change the overall architecture and design.

The iterative-only lifecycles excel at managing technical risk because the team and the customer work together, experimenting as they proceed.

4.6. Culture Challenges with an Iterative Lifecycle

Iterative lifecycles are supposed to have collaborative cross-functional teams. However, I've seen way too many iterative projects where one person directs the entire team's work. That person assigns work to individuals.

Then, because the team does not learn together, the WIP increases and people focus on "their" work, a resource efficiency culture.

Iterative lifecycle projects can change that tendency when they make shorter feedback loops and faster decisions. The more the team can focus on a small deliverable that offers information, the more these teams can start to manage themselves.

Iterative lifecycles address the need for product experimentation. In addition, when a team incorporates retrospectives when they complete a prototype, the team can learn from its work and inform the next piece of work.

However, because iterative lifecycles do not address delivery risk, they do not support management's need to manage the project portfolio. That's a trap for iterative-only teams. (That's one of the reasons I've seen so many UP teams move to an incremental approach, without iterating over feature sets.)

The slower the team is to deliver, the more likely the team will hear these questions or demands:

- What have you done for me lately?

- When can I expect anything?
- I need a delivery on such-and-such a date.

Those date-focused questions also reduce the team's consideration of technical excellence. That can create even later, unplanned feedback loops.

In the same way that I recommend you limit the time for a serial lifecycle project, I also recommend you limit an iterative-only project to six months. And if you use a UP, consider four-to-six-week release trains, not any longer.

The more often the project can release the product, the less other people will want to control the work.

4.7. Remember This About Iterative Lifecycles

Iterative lifecycles can excel at integrating customer feedback. If your project uses an iterative lifecycle, prepare your team for success with these tips:

1. Decide how you will treat your prototypes. Will you throw them away once you have customer feedback and redo the code? Or, are you supposed to build on the prototype? That answer will tell you how much refinement you will need to do before and after you show the customer.
2. These lifecycles depend on regular customer feedback. If you don't get that feedback, what will you do?
3. Before you start the project, decide how many changes or kinds of feedback your customer can offer. While the team wants to deliver something the customer will find useful, some customers take advantage of these lifecycles by asking for changes, ad nauseum. Make sure everyone agrees on the boundaries.

But with only one release at the end or with many-week release trains, the iterative lifecycles are not yet perfect. That's why we also have incremental lifecycles.

Chapter 5. Incremental Lifecycles

Both serial and many iterative approaches have only one release at the end of the project. That's fine if the team or the organization does not encounter any additional project or product risks.

However, I've seen these problems:

- The team realizes that after this set of features, the architecture won't support additional features.
- The product manager realizes the market is changing faster than the team can complete the entire project.
- Management decides they need to change the strategy, and this product no longer fits the new strategy.

Instead of losing all the created value, incremental lifecycles can allow teams to release what they completed up until now. Instead of having a lot of features in progress, the incremental lifecycles help teams finish something useful and release that. Then, everyone can choose their next decisions.

The incremental approaches optimize for schedule risk because they focus on more frequent deliveries throughout the project.

Those decisions might include stopping this project once the project has delivered enough capability. That's when the organization can see how the customers use the product and what the customers request before deciding on more work for the product. Or, the organization might cancel further work on the product. Or the organization plans when to end this product's life.

In all these cases, this project is done. That decision frees the team to work on other products. But all of those decisions depend on the release of a working product.

That's the beauty of an incremental lifecycle—especially when you plan for multiple interim releases. Those releases also allow—and encourage—the team to show their visible progress on a regular basis, even before a release.

That visible progress encourages feedback at the time of the demo, internal, or external release.

5.1. Incremental Approaches Are Not New

In 1975, Basili and Turner published "Iterative Enhancement: A Practical Technique for Software Development." [BAT75] That paper describes an incremental approach to validating the architecture as the team works through the feature sets. In addition, the paper uses the words, "skeletal implementation," similar to the idea of a "walking skeleton" that many agilists use now.

When my colleagues and I used these lifecycles back in the 70s, 80s, and 90s, we *tended* to complete one entire feature set at a time. I often chose to work on the riskiest feature sets, not the most valuable feature sets.

Now we know it's often better to rank by value.

I have used two different incremental lifecycles: Design to Schedule and Staged-Delivery.

5.2. Design to Schedule Focuses on Release Candidates

Many projects receive a ship-by date from their managers. And sometimes, managers change that ship date to something earlier than the team expected. If that ever happens to you, Design to Schedule might be a good choice, especially if you can't use an agile approach.

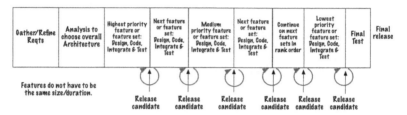

Figure 14. Design to Schedule

In this lifecycle, the team does some up-front planning. They gather or refine the requirements and then use those requirements to choose an overall architecture. Then, the team moves to the highest priority feature or feature set, doing all the design, code, integration, and testing for those highest priority features or feature sets.

The team completes an increment of value every time they finish a feature or feature set. While they don't *have* to release that increment externally, they can. That's why there's a "Release candidate" at the end of each feature set.

Design to Schedule allows the team to stop whenever they encounter the "we must ship what we have now" date. The project does not have to continue.

That's why late feedback in Design to Schedule might not be the project Kiss of Death. The team can release what they have, because they've completed work as they proceeded.

5.3. Late Feedback in Design to Schedule

Because Design to Schedule offers checkpoints of completed value, late feedback does not have the same consequences as it does in the serial or iterative lifecycles, as in the next figure.

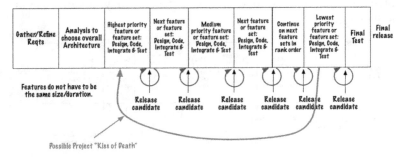

Figure 15. Feedback Loops in Design to Schedule

If the product leader and the team realize there is late feedback that might put the entire product at risk, they can decide to ship any of the previous release candidates. That removes the pressure on the team and allows them time to regroup and rethink what the product needs.

Sometimes, teams or product leaders need to plan interim deliveries. That's where the Staged Delivery lifecycle works quite well.

5.4. Staged Delivery Focuses on Multiple Releases

Design to Schedule offers an option to release. Staged Delivery assumes the team *will* release, as in the next figure.

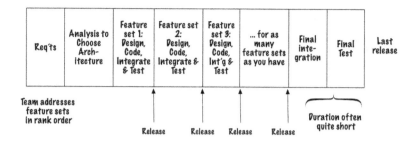

Figure 16. Staged Delivery

Staged Delivery starts with gathering requirements, in whatever way we choose. Someone, often a product leader, ranks the feature sets. The team chooses the most appropriate architecture, based on what they know now

Then, the team delivers a feature set to the customers. (If you have a hardware product, you might release internally for other people's consumption, but the idea is the team releases to customers where possible.)

Because the team releases a completed increment of value, management can stop the project. No one needs to tidy anything, because the team completed that increment's worth of work.

Assuming management wants the project to continue, the team works on another feature set and delivers it with another release.

The team continues implementing by feature and releasing. Sometimes, at the end of the project, there's one more small feature here and another over there. In that case, the team might need a final integration and a final test, but those tend to be very short in duration.

Late feedback feels very different in a Staged Delivery lifecycle.

5.5. Late Feedback in Staged Delivery

Feedback loops exist in Staged Delivery projects, too, as in the next figure.

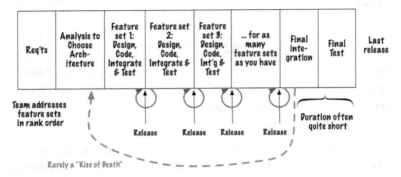

Figure 17. Staged Delivery Feedback Loops

The small circles are regular feedback loops, the kind that the team can manage. And the large and late feedback loop rarely turns into a project Kiss of Death.

That's because the team has released regularly throughout the entire project.

When I used Staged Delivery back in the 80s and 90s, we did not release the product every two weeks. However, we released internally at least once a week and externally as often as we could afford to release.

Late feedback prompts more conversations.

5.6. Learn from Late Feedback

Project teams learn from late feedback. However in incremental lifecycles because the team releases regularly, that learning does not create the same kind of project problems as in the serial or iterative lifecycles.

In addition, the team gains information and can reflect when they release. Releasing informs the next set of activities. For example, the team might:

- Iterate over prototypes, often as a new project.
- Create a new *product.* In my experience, several organizations chose to create Lite and Pro versions of their original product.
- Use a timeboxed set of experiments to decide what to do next.

Releasing isn't just for the customers. It's also for the team, for the product, and for the project portfolio. However, incremental lifecycles shine when there is more than one team involved, as on a program.

5.7. Programs Thrive With Incremental Approaches

A program consists of two or more projects that work to achieve a common business objective for one product or service. (See *Agile and Lean Program Management: Scaling Collaboration Across the Organization* [ROT16A] for more information about program management.)

Imagine a small program of three cross-functional teams. They're all on one project at the same time, but they work on different feature sets, as in the next figure.

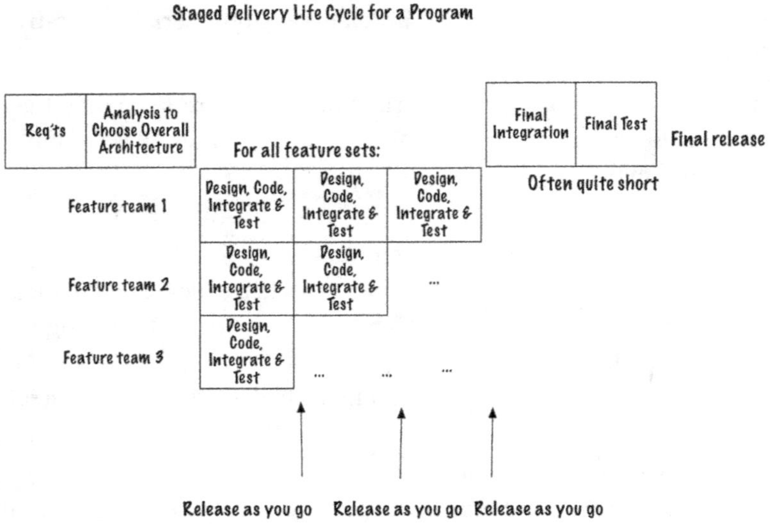

Staged Delivery Life Cycle for a Program

Req'ts	Analysis to Choose Overall Architecture	For all feature sets:			Final Integration	Final Test	Final release
Feature team 1		Design, Code, Integrate & Test	Design, Code, Integrate & Test	Design, Code, Integrate & Test	Often quite short		
Feature team 2		Design, Code, Integrate & Test	Design, Code, Integrate & Test	...			
Feature team 3		Design, Code, Integrate & Test	...	...	...		

Release as you go   Release as you go   Release as you go

Figure 18. Program-Level Staged Delivery

This is how I managed programs back in the 80s. Every team worked independently, and we released internally once a month. At that time, we released to customers on tape, and then CD, so the cost to release to customers was very high. However, we invited customers to come to our building and see demos on a regular basis. And because not every feature set took an entire month, we could show customers what we completed as soon as we completed the feature.

That's why short-duration release trains work so well.

5.8. Short-Duration Release Trains Focus on Finishing

In 1984, I was the solo programmer for an experimental product. It took me six weeks to finish that prototype and show my work. My manager (and all the various interested people) breathed a sigh of relief when I finally showed them a demo. They offered great feedback and I finished that prototype and handed it off to a product team.

I could have used that feedback earlier to inform the next bit of prototyping.

When I realized I'd left all these people wondering for six weeks, I decided to never do that again. From then on, I would either show a demo or release something at *least* once a month. That way, these people could see what I had—and had not—finished since the previous month.

I wasn't the only one using release trains. Sun published their release trains for years. Cisco still does now, for their IOS XE product. Several of my clients in the 1990s used release trains to good effect.

That's the point of a release train, a timebox that says, "We will always release on this day." That release cadence builds momentum in the team and builds trust with the various partners around the organization.

The shorter the timebox, that release train, the more focus the team can use to finish *this* batch of work.

Even with frequent releases, incremental lifecycles are not perfect at managing all the various risks.

5.9. Challenges for Incremental-Only Lifecycles

There's a huge element missing in the incremental lifecycles, especially if a project or program takes more than a few months to complete. That is the customer. (I ignored my customer too long in that story just above.)

While incremental lifecycles offer the opportunity to choose which feature set to do next, based on customer feedback, there's no expectation as part of the lifecycle to use customer feedback.

And if the team doesn't release often, the incremental lifecycle looks just like a serial lifecycle—except it puts more pressure on the team.

That said, the incremental lifecycles offer more agility than just iterative approaches.

5.10. Opportunities for Agility

Just as with the iterative lifecycles, incremental lifecycles require cross-functional teams who work together. It makes no sense to stagger developers and then testers. The team works together. That's how they can release every feature set.

And because the team releases (at minimum, internally) every time they finish a feature set, the team has these opportunities for agility:

- Re-rank the remaining feature sets. I've seen many product leaders re-order the rest of the work as soon as the team releases one feature or feature set.
- End the project whenever the product leader or management wants to. (This addresses schedule risk.)
- Gain early insight into architectural or other potential product risks.
- See and demo the product as it grows.
- Manage the project portfolio more easily because the project releases value more often. The people who make the portfolio decisions can decide whether to continue on this product or ask the team to move to another product.

If the team takes advantage of shorter feedback loops, they can plan for change. That planning allows them to either release the product as is—or to refactor more often. Either way, incremental approaches tend to allow the team more ease in changing the overall architecture and design.

The more often the team releases, the more options they have for their future product development.

5.11. Culture Challenges with an Incremental Lifecycle

The larger the effort, the less likely anyone will try to control the individual pieces in an incremental project, especially if the project or program releases something useful often.

However, some incremental projects and programs do *not* limit the requirements or the architecture time. That leads to the up-front work causing that "Big Design Up Front" problem, as in the serial lifecycles.

Projects and programs can manage that problem by using a release train or other cadence to deliver finished work.

Release trains say that on a time-based cadence, such as once every month or quarter, the team will deliver finished work on a particular day. When I used release trains back in the 1980s, we chose the 15th of the month and we released what we completed. One of my clients in the 1990s chose a train of once every two months.

Incremental lifecycles tend to encourage more collaboration, shorter feedback loops, and more frequent decision-making. However, if managers believe in resource efficiency, they will pressure the people to do "more," with the inevitable multitasking.

5.12. Remember This About Incremental Lifecycles

Incremental lifecycles excel at managing schedule risk because everyone expects to release something relatively frequently. And because the team releases as the project progresses, everyone can see how the product fits together, which allows for faster customer feedback.

Teams tend to keep the product "clean" because they expect to release more frequently. For example, teams often maintain all the various tests so the team can release as often as they finish a feature set.

If your project uses an incremental lifecycle, prepare the team for success with these ideas:

1. Release as often as possible. For example, consider a weekly cadence of internal releases and demos, with an external release every two weeks. If your product leader created a many-month-long backlog, the frequent releasing might ease some of the pressure that results from that backlog.
2. Maintain the tests as the team completes features, so the team can continue to release.
3. Consider when your project will invite customer feedback.

If your company can't create an agile culture, consider an incremental lifecycle, especially if you have schedule risks.

However, the incremental lifecycles don't address experimentation, so next up is the combination lifecycles. These are iterative and incremental lifecycles that do not require an agile culture to succeed.

Chapter 6. Combination Lifecycles

Teams need to address their project and product risks when they select a lifecycle. However, the pervasive risks so far arise from too-long or unplanned feedback loops and too-infrequent decisions.

Iterative lifecycles support frequent customer feedback to reduce the technical risks of not building what the customers want. Incremental lifecycles support frequent releases so everyone can choose what to do next.

However, no one is clairvoyant. That has several implications, even if the project driver, constraints, and floats remain the same:

- The need for innovation might change, even through one project.
- The requirements will change, especially if the project lasts longer than about six months.
- Those changes often alter what the product needs for architecture and design. As a result, the code and tests will need to change.

Even on a product with a moderate innovation need, a team will need to iterate over some requirements and provide more frequent releases so they can receive some feedback.

Your product might not need to release to the customer every two weeks for feedback. However, in my experience, releasing the product internally at least once a week—and preferably daily—will help everyone understand the product's progress.

Every time the customer sees the product, they might change their mind about what they need. Which sends us into more feedback loops for analysis, architecture, and design.

Worse, any increment of value that does not take the customers' needs into account will prevent future project progress. And any feature-based iterative approach that does not deliver something, sometime "soon," will prevent the product's success.

That's why all the project- and product-based risks outlined in Section 2.1: Lifecycles Manage Risks on page 13 have both tactical and strategic implications for the project, product, and organization.

And because feedback loops offer information about risks , most projects require some form of iterative and incremental approach. See Section 2.3: Project Tradeoffs Clarify Feedback Loops on page 15. The more you understand your project's risks, the better you can decide how much to iterate and when to deliver an increment of value.

Most projects require both iterative and incremental approaches. All projects can plan for that, although those plans will not fit into a nice, neat Gantt chart.

Most of the projects I encounter are date-driven. So let's start there.

6.1. A Date-Driven Combination Lifecycle

For years, I managed projects and programs where we needed to meet a specific release date. However, we still had technical risks, So this Date-Driven Combination Lifecycle worked well until I learned about agile approaches.

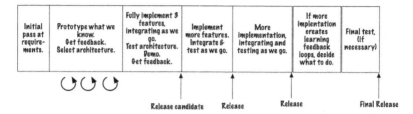

Initial pass at require- ments.	Prototype what we know. Get feedback. Select architecture.	Fully implement 3 features, integrating as we go. Test architecture. Demo. Get feedback.	Implement more features. Integrate & test as we go.	More implementation, integrating and testing as we go.	If more implentation creates learning feedback loops, decide what to do.	Final test, (if necessary)
			Release candidate	Release	Release	Final Release

Figure 19. Date-Driven Combination Lifecycle

Since serial lifecycles are notorious for "Requirements Hell," the first thing I did was to offer the product people a maximum of two weeks to gather and define requirements.

To be honest, that was probably too long, but that seemed a reasonable amount of time back then.

Why just two weeks?

First, it's impossible to ever fully define all the requirements for an innovative product. Second, the more innovation your customers want, the faster they will change their minds. As soon as the team delivers an increment of value, the customers will say, "Great! Now, can we have that thing over there?"

But the real reason to limit the requirements time is simple: The less time people spend on requirements gathering and definition, the more likely they are to focus on the essential requirements.

Especially if the project will iterate as the team learns and delivers increments of value, the product people don't need a lot of time to define the requirements in advance.

Next, the team prototyped a few important features, using Evolutionary Prototyping. Most of the time, the team decided which three features. I asked the team to keep their prototyping to a maximum of four weeks.

Four weeks was enough time for the team to focus on just the questions they needed to answer *and* show a prototype to other people.   At the end of the prototyping, the team selected the specifics of the product architecture.

In a serial lifecycle, that prototype would have been an architecture document. Then, various people might have reviewed the architecture. But a prototype allows a different form of architecture review. People can *see* the prototype in action.

Prototype What the User Sees

Sometimes, the user experience or the specific user interface can change the architecture. If you think that might happen in your product, consider these choices:

- Create a paper prototype of the user interface and describe which pieces may have architectural impact on the entire product.
- Walk reviewers through the major use cases for the product.
- Agree on a decision point in the near future to assess the user experience and the user interface.

In general, help everyone see where the user interface affects the product.

Then, using the architecture, the team fully implemented those three features. Most of the time, the team threw away their earlier prototypes, because they had learned so much from the prototyping work.

These three features might be all over the product, because the idea was to be able to verify the architecture would work for the product. That effort resulted in a release candidate.

The team demonstrated the release candidate to anyone who was interested, and definitely the product leader. If the product leader thought this release candidate was useful, the team released it.

All of the feedback loops so far allowed:

- The product leader to rank and re-rank the feature sets.
- The team to see the product and project risks and manage them.
- Management to build trust with the team because management could see visible progress.

Then, back in the 80s, we planned for the next month and released at the end of that month. (Our months were often not the literal end of the month, but sometime in the middle of the month, such as "the Tuesday closest to the 15th of the month.")

Because we tested the architecture, we didn't have too many late feedback loops. If we did, we chose what to do. Most of the time, we stopped *this* project and released what we had. Then we took the risks into the next project.

This approach uses the ideas of early iterations to "prove" the architecture and then move into increments of value.

But what if you aren't sure you can implement the product?

That's a combination lifecycle focused on Feature Sets.

6.2. A Feature-Set Driven Combination Lifecycle

A feature-set driven combination lifecycle addresses these technical risks:

- Whether or not the team *can* deliver the features in the desired time. (Is it possible for the team to create a product that fits these needs?)
- Whether the customers will want these features as the team implements them.

These questions require the team to iterate over the requirements much more than deliver incremental releases. However, the team does need to deliver more often than once during the project, to obtain various feedback.

Here's a feature-set combination lifecycle one of my clients used:

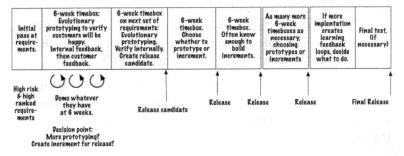

Initial pass at require-ments.	6-week timebox: Evolutionary prototyping to verify customers will be happy. Internal feedback, then customer feedback.	6-week timebox on next set of requirements: Evolutionary prototyping. Verify internally. Create release candidate.	6-week timebox. Choose whether to prototype or increment.	6-week timebox. Often know enough to build increments.	As many more 6-week timeboxes as necessary, choosing prototypes or increments	If more implentation creates learning feedback loops, decide what to do.	Final test, (if necessary)

High risk & high ranked require-ments

Demo whatever they have at 6 weeks.

Release candidate

Release   Release   Release   Final Release

Decision point:
More prototyping?
Create increment for release?

Figure 20. Feature Driven Combination Lifecycle

This client used a series of six-week timeboxes to manage the size and number of the features. From experience, they knew that most teams could deliver three to four small features in a feature set in six weeks.

If the team was ready before the six-week mark, they asked for internal feedback. Depending on the kind of product, they either did a limited release to selected customers or asked the customers to watch a demo.

They liked this approach because the team felt "just enough" pressure to work quickly, but not so much pressure that they cut corners. They had enough time to experiment with the prototypes.

Once the team finished prototyping, they moved to an incremental lifecycle, delivering value every six weeks.

While I might prefer a shorter timebox than six weeks, this approach worked for them for many years. (They have since moved to an agile approach with two-week timeboxes, because their culture was ready for them to do so.)

This client said they never had "late" feedback loops. Since they kept their projects small—under nine months—I suspect they were correct.

Their customized approach worked well for them.

6.3. Customize Your Own Combination Approach

I've offered two specific combination lifecycles here. However, you can customize your project's approach. Remember:

- The more exploration the features need, the more the team needs to iterate over feature sets. That is, address several features in one feature set and either prototype or finish them. In addition, consider which feature sets the team needs to explore and when.
- The more risky the date is, the more often the team needs to practice delivering value.

And if your project's and product's risks change as the team proceeds, you can always use what the team learned to inform the next bit of planning. That increases the team's agility.

6.4. Combination Lifecycles Offer More Agility

These lifecycles offer projects more agility than either iterative or incremental lifecycles because they:

- Focus on the customers and what the customers need.
- Limit the WIP, so the team isn't trying to juggle all the requirements at once.
- Request that the team collaborate to finish the work.

One savvy project manager said, "And we can't use a Gantt chart at the start of this project. That's a real win!"

Even though combination lifecycles require some initial planning, they also require frequent replanning. That's why a Gantt chart isn't often useful for the team.

When I used these approaches, I made a list of major milestones, such as when we needed to see which features in a demo, and when to start beta testing. I then offered that list to the team and to management. Then, the team and I used rolling wave planning to plan for the next month in detail. (Now, a product leader is more likely to make that list of milestones.)

In addition, if the teams uses short feedback loops, they can manage for change, which allows more frequent refactoring and the ability to alter the architecture and design without too many headaches.

6.5. Programs Thrive With Combination Approaches

I already said that incremental approaches work well for programs.

However, I know of too many programs where the projects are the "development" project and the "testing" project. Instead of cross-functional teams that collaborate, the developers and testers work separately. Yes, this violates the idea of cross-functional collaboration, but some organizations still work like this.

Component teams can rarely achieve an agile culture because they focus on resource efficiency. (See Section 1.3: Resource Efficiency Creates an Anti-Agility Culture on page 5.)

Consider this combination approach, either of a date-driven or feature-driven lifecycle if you have component teams.

When team members work as separate functions, inevitably, some function does not have sufficient time to finish "all" their work. A combination approach might help that program's agility, as in the next figure.

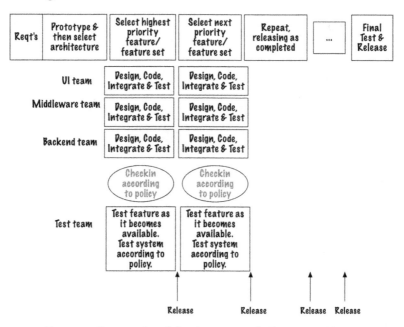

Figure 21. Program-Level Combination with Component Teams

With component teams, everyone has to agree on specific policies for faster feedback loops and more frequent decisions:

- Check-in policy: How often will each team check their code or tests into the version control system? Even with component teams, I like each team to check in their code at least once a day, if not more often.
- Build policy: The more often teams check in their code, the more feedback they can offer each other. And, the more frequently they can build the product. For me, a daily build is the least often—I prefer builds much more often. When teams feel the need to build more frequently, they tend to make their features smaller.
- Feature test policy: While component teams might work on features, no feature is complete until all the teams complete the feature. However, component teams rarely implement through the architecture. See Section 3.6.1: Implement Across the Architecture, Not Through on page 36. Because it's not possible to synchronize component teams, testing can't start until the last component team finishes their work.
- System test policy: In my experience, component teams tend to introduce errors that feature teams do not. That's because a single feature team takes responsibility for a given feature. However, component teams share that responsibility. To manage those risks, I recommend a program of component teams explicitly state how often the test team and the other teams will test the entire product.

Component teams look like they subscribe to a Concurrent Engineering philosophy. They do not because the people across the components are not collaborating to deliver features through the architecture.

While a combination lifecycle can help a cross-functional team, these lifecycles might not help component teams. That's one of the challenges of a combination lifecycle.

6.6. Challenges for Combination Lifecycles

When teams decide when to prototype and when to release, they can optimize how they manage the risks of customer feedback and the various decision-making. Combination lifecycles can allow teams to prototype in the middle of a project or a program, especially if the team(s) need to get fast customer feedback.

Here are challenges to review with your team or program:

- Decide how long to prototype. The longer the prototypes take, the less feedback the team has from the customer.
- Consider a cadence of releasing. I like—at a minimum—weekly internal releases, with a minimum of a monthly release.
- Watch for component teams instead of cross-functional teams. Component teams can create a kind of finishing "hell," where most of the components are done, but one part of the feature or feature set is stuck inside one team. No one can tell when that or any team can finish. (See Section 3.2.3: Unplanned Feedback Loops Create Unpredictability on page 31.)

Combination lifecycles still have culture challenges, too.

6.7. Culture Challenges with a Combination Lifecycle

Combination lifecycles support more experimentation and more delivery than any other lifecycle so far. For example, your team might decide they want to spend the first three weeks prototyping across the product, and then deliver those increments of value for another three weeks.

Or, your team might know exactly what the customers want now, but will have to experiment later.

The more the team chooses how it will work, the more agile the team is, especially if they add a retrospective at regular intervals.

However, I've seen these control problems with combination lifecycle teams:

- Someone outside the team demands the team "commit" to a large and long backlog of work, assuming the team does not need to experiment.
- The managers assign an architect who does not know how to work iteratively and incrementally, which means that person wants to define the architecture up front.
- Even if the people want, they have no opportunity to create cross-functional teams instead of component teams.

Component teams tend to create a serial lifecycle, even if the project or program decides it wants a combination approach. That's because some person or team is always waiting for some other person or team to complete their work because they can release, internally or externally.

6.8. Remember This About Combination Lifecycles

If your team or program can't use an agile approach, a combination lifecycle can help manage your project's and product's risks.

If your project or program uses a combination lifecycle, prepare the team(s) for success with these ideas:

1. Decide which features require prototypes and when. Know how you will get customer feedback.
2. Release as often as possible. For example, consider a weekly cadence of internal releases and demos, with an external release every two weeks. If your product leader created a many-month-long backlog, the frequent releasing might ease some of the pressure that results from that backlog.
3. Maintain the tests as the team completes features, so the team can continue to release.

Combination lifecycles have a lot in common with agile approaches. But just because these lifecycles are iterative and incremental does not mean they are agile approaches.

Agile approaches are different.

Chapter 7. Agile Approaches

Agility requires culture changes to manage the team, product, and management needs and risks. (See Section 1.1: Visualize a Successful Agile Team Culture on page 2 for more details. But an agile culture is not sufficient.

While each agile team is unique, each agile team has similar characteristics.

7.1. Characteristics of an Agile Team

All agile teams, regardless of their approach, have these characteristics in common:

- The team limits its WIP.
- The team defaults to collaboration over solo work.
- Regularly, the team delivers value, at least internally, if not to an external customer.
- The team realizes that while features might be done for now, the requirements, architecture, and user experience are not done until this version of the product ships.
- The team retrospects and considers what to do for continuous improvement.

When teams work like this, they work in flow efficiency, controlling their work themselves.

Because they release and retrospect, they have many fewer unplanned feedback loops. These characteristics allow the team to manage its project, product, and portfolio risks.

That's it.

Teams choose practices that allow them to create their specific agile culture. One team might use iterations (a short timebox) to manage its WIP over a one- to two-week period. A different team might create WIP limits for the overall team.

Some teams do both because they learned that just limiting overall WIP doesn't work because they have a tendency for work to accumulate in one area. (That accumulation tends to occur where the team does not have sufficient skills and capabilities to finish the work.)

However, when teams choose to collaborate on a given feature, the team delivers value as early as possible. That delivery allows the product leader to assess the feedback inside and outside the organization, selecting the next bit of work.

The earlier the team can deliver the value, the fewer unplanned feedback loops anyone encounters. That value allows the team to recognize that feedback might cause changes to the requirements, architecture, and user experience.

That is, the team recognizes the requirements, architecture, and user experience cannot be "complete" until the product ships.

Why Specify User Experience as Incomplete?

You might agree with me that an agile approach acknowledges the requirements and architecture will change. But the user experience, too?

Many product leaders specify the user experience inside the requirements document, regardless of the lifecycle. I've never understood that because as the customers see the product, they ask for changes in the user experience and the requirements.

Instead of trying to specify the user experience, product leaders can specify the *goals* of that experience. Then, as everyone processes the internal and external feedback, the product leader can check the goals and see if the older goals align with the product evolution. Creating an incremental approach to the user experience works exactly the same way as the architecture. See Section 7.2.1: Coherent Product Architectures Emerge from the Work on page 92. The user experience emerges from the work.

That early and often delivery has other benefits. The team doesn't just learn from internal or customer feedback. The team also can take a little time to learn from how they worked and how they felt about that work.

Because agile teams limit their WIP and collaborate, they can create short feedback loops for delivery and learning. Or, they use their short feedback loops to reduce WIP and increase collaboration. That's a restatement of Little's Law.

Agile teams also visualize their work with a team board and with value stream maps.

7.1.1. Team Boards Visualize Progress

Since so many teams start their agile journey with Scrum, they often start with a three-column Scrum board as in the next figure.

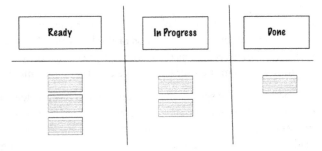

Figure 22. Three-Column Scrum Board

That board is terrific if you can keep your cycle time low and if the team collaborates on the work. Notice that this board has only two items in the In Progress column. So this team is collaborating and finishing.

But too often, I see teams who are supposed to use an agile approach but don't have the necessary people on their team, such as enough testers. Or, the team is also supposed to do production support.

Whatever the issue, their work gets stuck somewhere in the In Progress column. And they don't know where.

That's when teams might want a different board to explicitly show how work flows through their team. Six months ago, one of my clients used a Kanban board like the one in the next image to show their system of work.

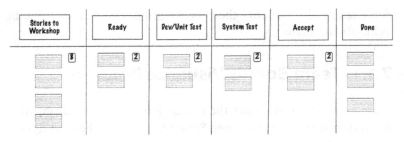

Figure 23. Multiple Column Kanban Board

One team on its agile journey decided to focus on lowering WIP in their current state. They had a significant number of production support interruptions from a previous release. They wanted to integrate fixes with their current product development and avoid an Urgent or Expedite lane.

They chose to collaborate in twos or threes, either pairing or swarming on one item at a time. Only the product leader did not collaborate. That's because she was overloaded, supposedly working with two other teams as their product leader.

Read this board from the right side to the left to fully understand it.

This team decided to wait for four items to trigger a demo and a retrospective. Since their typical cycle time ran between one and three days, they tended to demo and retrospect every couple of weeks. (They also reviewed their throughput and tracked the age of all items as in Section 1.4.1: Measures Change in Flow Efficiency on page 7.)

To the left of Done is the Accept column. The reason the team has a WIP limit here is that the product leader will interrupt what she's doing to accept stories. She asked for that WIP limit so she doesn't get behind.

The remaining columns are also full. When I asked the team why they didn't have any slack in their system, one of them said, "We're still learning how to be most effective together. We keep experimenting with how we pair and swarm. We're thinking about mobbing/ensembling on the work, but not everyone is ready for that. But we know we need to keep our WIP low and we know we need to keep our cycle time low to manage our interruptions."

The only column that's not full is the Stories to Workshop column. Some teams create a cadence for workshopping stories. This team has a limit because their product leader wanted to workshop stories that they wouldn't add to a backlog for months. Instead of starting all that work, the Stories to Workshop column is a near-term roadmap or backlog.

This team controls how they work. Even so, the team has a full board, due to the previous culture of resource efficiency.

Six months later, that team changed its board. Because the product leader only works with this team, they no longer need WIP limits on the Accept column. In addition, the team rarely pairs, but works in triads. That allowed them to combine Dev/Unit Test and System Test into one column called Dev and Test.

Every agile team deserves a board that fits their current work and that they can use as a basis for experimentation. If your project has technical risks, your board might need to have a column for prototypes or experimentation. That's why the project, product, and organizational risks can change the approach a team can use.

Consider these questions for your board:

- Do we have enough information from our current board? If not, what else do we need?
- Do we need board-based WIP limits? Or, do we need column-based WIP limits?
- Do we have a policy about WIP limits? That is, do we allow ourselves to exceed them?

Boards aren't the only visualization that can help teams. Value stream maps can help a team visualize and isolate delays and bottlenecks.

7.1.2. Value Stream Maps Help Teams Visualize Problems

A value stream map shows two kinds of time: work time and wait time. The cycle time is the addition of the work time and the wait time, as in this figure.

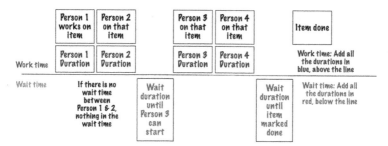

Cycle time = Work time plus Wait time. Consider rounding the total cycle time to half-day increments, not less.

Figure 24. Blank Value Stream Map

When teams estimate, they often do a reasonable job estimating the work time. But very few people or teams estimate the wait time accurately. Teams who work cooperatively, but primarily alone, always have a longer cycle time than teams who collaborate.

When managers believe in resource efficiency, cooperative team members tend to be busy all the time. However, the team can't finish any *item* faster.

Collaborative teams work together, keeping their WIP low. That means they tend to have much less wait time for any of the items.

This is why teams need to see and manage their cycle times as a trend. When a team changes something—even if they only change their board—they might change their cycle time trends. When teams learn their tendencies for cycle time, they can choose how to work better. And they can offer 50%, 80%, or 90% confidence levels for future predictions.

Agile approaches are deceptively easy-looking—unless your organization has a culture of extreme resource efficiency. But fake agility thrives because of the necessary changes to the culture and the team characteristics.

Teams, managers—everyone has questions.

7.2. Questions About How to Make Agility Work

When I teach teams and managers about how to work in an agile way, everyone asks these questions:

- If we don't do a lot of upfront design, how can we create a coherent product architecture?
- What if it's too risky for our customers to take the next release?
- How can we possibly predict when we will be done?
- We need a project manager. Why does this notion of "agile team" not include a project manager?

Some teams also ask, "Should we use Scrum or a Kanban system and how do we decide?"

These are valid questions because non-agile teams managed these risks with iterative, incremental, and combination lifecycles for years.

I'll start with the idea of creating a coherent product architecture when the team iterates over the requirements and delivers incrementally.

7.2.1. Coherent Product Architectures Emerge from the Work

Many of the unplanned feedback loops arise from significant architecture, requirements, or user experience changes late in the project. Those changes cascade back and forth, where one feature during testing causes a requirements change that then causes an architecture change, that causes a user experience change, and so on.

Anyone who's lived through any of these unplanned feedback loops knows how irritating and crazy-making they are. The unplanned feedback loops create project death marches with plenty of project and product risks.

Sometimes, teams can catch those changes in prototypes, but in my experience, the larger the feature set the team selects, the more likely they don't see the changes until late in the project. That's because many requirements and architectural changes emerge from how the various feature sets work together.

The more often the team can deliver a user-visible single story or small feature, the faster the team can see when they need to change the architecture or the requirements.

One alternative is to create a candidate architecture and test that, as in the incremental lifecycles. That can work, as long as the team is ready to release and then decide what to do in the next project.

An even better way is to *expect* change and manage the project and product to relatively easily incorporate those changes. There are several technical ways to manage this change:

- Use Behavior-Driven Development, where the team always uses an example to clarify the upcoming work,
- Refactor as the team completes a specific story, and
- Plan to use iterative and incremental architecture.

This way of thinking about agile architecture has several implications, especially for an architect. When teams move to trying something in the code and then releasing that, everyone practices architecture. There is no one person *responsible* for the architecture. Instead, that architect is now responsible for facilitating the team's thinking.

That's a form of servant leadership. Very few organizations reward architects (and other senior people) for their facilitation of other people's learning. That's one of the problems with resource efficiency thinking. See Section 1.3: Resource Efficiency Creates an Anti-Agility Culture on page 5. When organizations reward senior people for how they aid other people's learning, the team learns faster. And sometimes, the entire organization learns faster.

The faster the team moves to trying something in the code and then releasing that code for someone's feedback, the faster the team will discover if the architecture is coherent—and that the product offers value.

But fast releasing is not for all customers all the time.

7.2.2. Our Customers Can't Take Releases Fast

There's a difference between releasing *inside* the organization and releasing to customers. When I'm working on a product, I want to see at least one release every day.

But customers can't always take daily, weekly or monthly releases. For example, if you offer a tax product, customers might not be able to take a new release the day or week before everyone has to file their taxes. Depending on the rules, the customers might not want anything for a month or more after filing.

However, if you have *fixes*, your customers might want that new release before tax day. It all depends on the product and the customers.

When the team releases inside the organization, as often as possible, the team sees its progress. And the more demos they do, with or for other people, the more feedback they will receive from interested people across the organization.

But no one can offer feedback unless the team releases as often as possible. That frequent releasing reduces the need to answer this question: When will the product be done?

7.2.3. Our Managers Want Us to Predict Completion

It's not possible to predict when the team will complete the product. It might be possible for the team to predict with some amount of certainty when the team will finish something in the next week or so. But even if teams finish something every day, no one can predict a power outage or an internet outage. Outages will affect any dates, including a delivery date.

Other issues can affect a delivery date, such as production support issues that the team needs to address right now. Or the prototype worked fine, but the production-level implementation does not have the necessary speed. Or the regulations changed on some other piece of the product, such as privacy, so the team has to stop their current work and do that emergency or interrupting work instead.

Managers often ask when the project will be done because their experience means they can't really trust the team to deliver. These managers want to trust the team. But they've rarely seen a team deliver anything they promised "on time."

Teams who meet the agile characteristics and work in flow efficiency can make an informed prediction about when they might deliver something in the next few weeks. That's because those teams measure their cycle time, keep their WIP low, and regularly release internally. Couple that with frequent demos and other people realize they can trust the team.

But here's my prediction: Even a team whose cycle time is low and does not vary much cannot predict when they will have an unforeseen problem or risk. That makes any predictability far into the future a waste of everyone's time. (See *Predicting the Unpredictable: Pragmatic Approaches to Estimating Project Cost or Schedule* [ROT15] for more information.)

Maybe, up until now, the team has had a project manager to deal with the people outside the team. And while I've discussed projects and teams, I haven't yet discussed a project manager. That's because an agile project manager plays a totally different role than a project manager on a more traditional project. A team might need an agile project manager, but they might not.

7.2.4. Agile Project Management Changes from Control to Facilitation

In resource efficiency cultures, the people do not choose their work—someone often assigns it. Worse, someone often assigns that work and then tells that person how long the work will take. The person is supposed to deliver that work "on time."

That's a control, resource efficiency culture.

Instead, a team might need an agile project manager—but not to assign work or tell people how to work. Instead, an agile project manager facilitates the team's environment. I've seen the environment include:

- Eliminating other people's requests that team members multitask. This often arises from insufficient project portfolio management.
- Ensuring the product leader is available to the team on a regular basis. Too often, a single product leader is supposed to shepherd the business value of several products or feature sets at one time. The product leader is too overloaded to be available to any of those teams.
- Facilitating the project charter, including the project trade-offs, the product goal, and the overall release criteria. Again, the product leader might be overloaded or not realize they need to do this.

Agile project management means the project manager creates an agile culture so the team can succeed. That's because agile teams control their own work, often in collaboration with a product leader. The product leader shepherds the business value of the work the team will do now, next, and never. The team decides how they will work to deliver that value.

Agile Project Managers Might Be Scrum Masters and Vice Versa

The current iteration (2023) of the Scrum Guide [1] explains that the Scrum Master focuses on creating better Scrum in the team and for the organization. That's different than the facilitative role I describe in this book.

In my experience, management doesn't give a hoot about better Scrum. Management cares about releasing products that work. You can change what Scrum Masters and agile project managers do to succeed in your organization. Review your organization's culture and see what makes sense for any project-based leader.

Agile teams work with their product leader daily. Sure, there might be times when the product leader is out of the office, but an agile team requires a product leader to work with the team so they can collaborate on how to manage the team's WIP, when to experiment inside and with customers, and when it makes sense to deliver finished value.

Agile teams are collaborative, self-directed teams. They watch the flow of their work so they can deliver.

Agile product leaders balance the current product needs with their vision of the future. And as part of that collaborative team, plan a

---

[1] https://www.scrum.org/resources/scrum-guide

little now, get a little feedback, and then replan a little more.

Agile managers create a culture of options or bets. Instead of demanding a team (or many teams) deliver a product on a certain date, they watch the demos and monitor customer feedback from the various releases. These managers focus on creating a collaborative culture, so the team can keep its WIP low and its throughput high.

That's why agility is a cultural change.

7.3. Scrum, Kanban, or Some Combination?

First, let's see what an agile approach looks like, as in the next figure.

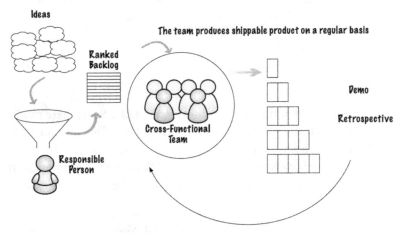

Figure 25. General Agile Picture

A responsible person, who I call the product leader, collects all the ideas floating around in the organization and creates a limited, ranked backlog for the cross-functional team. That team chooses the highest-rank work, finishes it, and creates an increment of value. That increment is "shippable" if someone can consume it.

On a regular basis, the team demonstrates its work, and conducts a retrospective to learn from what they did. At some point, after the team demos and retrospects, they get more work from the backlog.

Some teams use an iteration-based approach, as in the next figure.

Requirements Analysis Design Build Test Release Deploy	Requirements Analysis Design Build Test Release Deploy	Requirements Analysis Design Build Test Release Deploy	Requirements Analysis Design Build Test Release Deploy	Repeat as needed ...	Requirements Analysis Design Build Test Release Deploy	Requirements Analysis Design Build Test Release Deploy

Each timebox is the same size. Each timebox results in running tested features.

Figure 26. Iteration-Based Agile Approach

Scrum is the most famous of all the iteration-based agile approaches. Iterations are one- to four-week timeboxes called "sprints." By definition, when the timebox finishes, the team finishes that iteration.

Other teams use a flow-based approach, known as a Kanban system, as in the next figure.

Feature: Clarify Req't. Analysis Design Build Test Release Deploy	Feature: Clarify Requirement, Analysis Design Build Test Release Deploy	Feature: Clarify Requirement, Analysis Design Build Test Release Deploy	Repeat as needed ...	Feature: Clarify Requirement, Analysis Design Build Test Release Deploy	Feature: Clarify Requirement, Analysis Design Build Test Release Deploy

In flow, the team limits the number of features active at any time with WIP limits for each team activity.
There is no timeboxing built into flow.
The team does not specifically size the work.

Figure 27. Flow-Based Agile Approach

And of course, some teams like to use flow approaches inside a two-week iteration. In each case, the team takes a limited amount of work (WIP), delivers something useful for feedback, and then gets more work.

If the cost to release externally is too high, releasing internally for a while might be fine. The more often a team can release, the faster the team can get feedback. The fast feedback loops reduce many of the risks.

That's why, as long as the team exhibits the characteristics, see Section 7.1: Characteristics of an Agile Team on page 85, either approach, or both together, can work:

- The team limits its WIP. That means the team also needs control over their board so they can experiment with how they represent their work and their WIP limits.
- The team uses cycle time to estimate or assess the size of an item, so they're using real data for prediction. That cycle time data helps the team realize when the item sizes are too large, or if people are not collaborating enough.

Scrum can work well when the team focuses on one product at a time, and a minimum of interrupting work, such as production support. But if your team is supposed to manage an unpredictable amount of support requests and perform product development work, I recommend a Kanban system.

Worse, if your team is supposed to multitask on more than one product *and* do product support, I only recommend a Kanban system.

In addition, I recommend every agile team use flow metrics, so everyone can see the WIP, cycle time, aging, and throughput. (See Section 1.4.1: Measures Change in Flow Efficiency on page 7 for more details.)

Agility is not limited to software projects. Hardware projects can use agile approaches, too. It all depends on the cost of release.

7.4. Agile Products that Include Hardware

I've worked on products that included software, firmware, and hardware. All of them could use iterative and incremental approaches up until the time the product had to move to physical form, in the form of a pilot to customers.

Before that pilot, the various teams could iterate using prototypes, as in the Chapter 4: Iterative Lifecycles on page 49. The prototypes allowed the teams, including the hardware teams, to show their progress. Some of the hardware teams showed their progress on breadboards, but the prototypes allowed them to demonstrate progress.

As long as all the teams demonstrated their progress on a regular basis not longer than a month in duration, the product benefited from that iterative and incremental approach.

Other programs used some of the Chapter 6: Combination Lifecycles on page 71, where they released the software and firmware regularly, only viewed the hardware progress in a lab, and did not release the final hardware product until the end of the program. While the visual progress helped, most of us were concerned about how the customers would respond. But sometimes, the cost of interim releases are too high for customer-based feedback.

In *Agile and Lean Program Management: Scaling Collaboration Across the Organization* [ROT16A], I recommended the program use kanban boards, frequent demos, and continuous integration for all the work.

That continuous integration includes continuous design review. That design review and frequent integration—even if that integration only exists in a lab—offers short feedback loops.

One of the big risks for a hardware product is that the hardware development runs on a different cycle than the software development. Mechanical and firmware components often run on yet different cycles of development. I have not found an iteration-based approach that is useful for the overall program. Instead, I recommend either a biweekly cadence or a monthly release train to visualize the entire product.

Iteration vs. Cadence

An iteration is a timebox for the work. Many Scrum teams choose a two-week iteration, and know they will finish something useful in that time.

A cadence is more of a metronome or a drumbeat for the team or the program. When teams know they will demo something every Wednesday at noon, they might not worry as much about "how much can we do in an iteration." Instead, they might ask, "What will we demo for this next Wednesday?"

If your team has trouble reducing its WIP, consider using a weekly cadence for a demo, and not worry so much about a two-week iteration. When teams shorten their time horizon, they can reduce their cycle time and reduce their unplanned feedback loops.

Hardware agility is not new. While the cost to release often prevents "full" agility, as in releasing something to the customers every week or two, many hardware projects use agile ideas.

Very few construction projects create a full schedule upfront—because they know they will discover something in the ground or in the previous structure. In New England, where I live, many road construction projects only plan for the next mile, while they keep the entire goal in mind.

Agile approaches, with iterative planning and replanning, and incremental deliveries with feedback allow teams to learn as they proceed. That's a great way to reduce risks in product development.

7.5. Remember This About Agile Approaches

The more risks your project and product has, the more an agile approach will help you deliver something useful. Those deliveries allow you to manage risks better than early and long planning will.

However, agile approaches require a culture change to flow efficiency thinking and team changes that focus on the four flow metrics.

All agile approaches have this in common:

1. Limit WIP at all levels—for people, the team, and the product. WIP kills projects and products and creates enormous risks. High WIP increases cycle time, which puts everyone under pressure to deliver.
2. Team-based collaboration to manage cycle time. Agile teams who measure their cycle time can spot trends and decide how best to work. When teams visualize their cycle time, they tend to make better decisions.
3. Frequent delivery—at least, internally—for feedback. Agile teams shorten their feedback loops for faster learning. That helps them choose what to do next and how to do it.
4. Agile teams retrospect often, so they can continue to improve.

If you realize your culture will not allow anything other than fake agility, use the guidelines in the next chapter to create agile opportunities in your project.

7. Remember This About Agile

Chapter 8. Increase Agility in Any Approach

No one cares about a team's agility—with the possible exception of the team itself. But managers and customers do care about better products. The managers care when the team can release those products—that's why managers use capitalization metrics. And the customers care about the value those products offer.

The more agile the approach, the faster the team can deliver value to the customers—without late learning. That's why more agility in product development matters.

Since each product has its own innovation risks, the more a team plans for more frequent feedback loops and decision points, the more agility the team will have.

That's why unplanned feedback loops kill efforts and make everyone's lives worse. Intentional feedback loops allow a team to manage project and innovation risks. Those intentional feedback loops help the team and the various leaders recover from earlier decisions.

That's why agile approaches—assuming your culture allows them—work so well. They offer frequent loops and decision points.

We know these two facts about organizational culture:

- We need a culture that focuses on the flow of work to successfully use an agile approach. Too few cultures do that. See Section 1.4: Flow Efficiency Creates an Agile Culture on page 6 for more details.

- Worse, we know that agility dies in a resource-efficiency culture.

I have yet to see managers start by changing the culture. However, if you want more agility in your project or team, focus on reducing the number and duration of unplanned feedback loops.

What would have to be true to reduce unplanned feedback loops in your organization?

8.1. Tips to Reduce Unplanned Feedback Loops

In serial lifecycles, unplanned feedback loops arise from an overemphasis on planning when everyone knows the least about the product. In the other lifecycles, unplanned feedback loops arise when the team waits too long to demo or release to a customer for feedback.

What would have to be true for your organization to plan less upfront, demo more frequently, and release often?

Consider these tips:

- Timebox all phases or up-front work. I recommend a maximum of two weeks for each phase.
- Deliver something at least as often as every month, at least internally, if not to a customer.
- Start the project with a cross-functional team that stays together for the entire project.

Here's how each of these tips can work.

8.1.1. Timebox Any Phase to Two Weeks

Timeboxes work for several reasons. The first is that everyone knows it's not possible to do *all* the requirements, architecture, customer experience, high-level design, and anything else in two weeks. That means no one fools themselves into thinking any of those phases are "done" or "complete."

That builds iteration into the project.

In addition, imagine if your project limited all the up-front work to just six weeks. Then, if people worked as a collaborative team, they could deliver something often, even if that's just a demo. The more often everyone—leaders, managers, and the team—sees that product growing, the more likely the team can stay together for the entire project.

I'm not guaranteeing those consequences from timeboxing the early phases. But they are certainly more likely. All because the early up-front work did not take forever.

Maybe you're in the middle of a project and you've already spent that time. Now, it's time to deliver something on a regular basis.

8.1.2. Deliver and Demo on a Regular Cadence

Back in my math classes, my teachers always said to "show your work." They didn't mean a document—they meant my math, how I worked through the problem.

That's why I recommend every team deliver something as often as possible. If the team can't deliver something daily, can they deliver weekly? If not weekly, how about every two weeks? At a minimum, a team needs to deliver something monthly so *they* can show their work to themselves, to see their progress.

When a project has to deliver something on a regular basis, the team tends to change how it works. The people realize they need to accommodate inevitable changes in the requirements, the architecture, the user experience, and certainly, the code and tests. If they know about Figure 1: Little's Law on page 8, they will finish one item before they start another. They will keep their WIP low and create higher throughput. And finishing means all the tests and necessary technical excellence for what they know now.

The team might realize they need a new board, one that shows each item's state, so they can finish as much as possible.

While I like daily or more frequent releases, some teams can't even imagine a monthly release train. If your team is like that, explain that releasing something every month isn't a goal to release *everything*. Instead, it's a goal to finish something valuable and release that.

Then, introduce the idea of a strong cadence of releases: monthly, biweekly, or weekly, regardless of whether you call it a train. At that release, the team demonstrates what they finished since the previous release.

A cadence of releases manages several risks. If the team misses a cadence, they know their WIP is too high or any given item is too large—or both. In addition, a cadence allows a team to use the work they completed to inform the next bit of work or planning.

Too many teams do not have sufficient test or release infrastructure to deliver something every week. In that case, work on that project first. It will save you time in the not-too-long run.

Ask your team, "What would have to happen for us to create a strong and short cadence of releases?" The team might say:

- We'd have to finish what we start.
- We'd have to increase collaboration because our WIP is too high.
- We need the ability to release ourselves, not rely on any other team.

Your team might have other options. Start from the goal of reducing unplanned feedback loops and see what the team thinks.

Many teams realize they need one cross-functional team that stays together for the entire project.

8.1.3. Use a Cross-Functional Team for the Entire Project

Back in 1993, Christopher Meyer published *Fast Cycle Time: How to Align Purpose, Strategy, and Structure for Speed* [MEY93]. That was the first book I read about concurrent engineering and the need for cross-functional teams. He used the term, "multifunctional," which is a great term for teams with all the skills and capabilities they need.

Concurrent engineering, where the phases span the entire project with cross-functional teams is an old idea. When I started to teach project management in the early 1990s, I explained the idea that freeze or complete was a pipe dream. See Section 3.2.2: Freeze or Complete Never Occurs on page 31. We "froze" or "completed" when we shipped the product. And with a cross-functional team, projects could reduce their risks of late and unplanned feedback loops.

If you start your project with a cross-functional team that has all the capabilities and skills it needs, and you retain that team with zero multitasking, your project can avoid many of the unplanned feedback loops. And the faster that team will learn.

Even if you must use phases or gates, the testers will ask questions during the requirements phase which will clarify the requirements. The designers and testers will clarify the architecture and high-level design with their questions.

Product development speed is about the speed of a *team's* learning. Maximize that speed with that cross-functional team from Day One. In addition, add retrospectives to a cadence of deliveries.

8.1.4. Learn with Retrospectives

Ask yourself or your team this question: When was the last time your team conducted a retrospective on how you worked?

Teams who take advantage of a cadence of delivery to *also* use a cadence of learning, tend to learn faster. That faster learning can help a team reduce its unplanned feedback loops.

If you're facilitating the retrospective, make sure to help the team learn about its technical practices, not just its project practices or product planning.

Once you reduce the unplanned feedback loops, consider how you can support a more collaborative culture.

8.2. Pursue a More Collaborative Culture

Agility requires a culture of collaboration. And people do what the organization rewards. However, you might be able to start to nudge your current culture to a more collaborative one with these ideas:

- Measure the flow metrics to see the project's reality.
- Plan for shorter projects, to release something faster and more frequently.
- Use rolling wave planning to plan to replan.

Let's start with the flow metrics.

8.2.1. Use Flow Metrics to See Reality

Flow metrics show the actual project and product data. They show you what the team completed and what's in progress. They show the reality much more reliably than traditional project measures. That's because Little's Law always wins. See Section 1.4.1: Measures Change in Flow Efficiency on page 7 for more information. Here's how the flow metrics work together:

- The higher the WIP, the lower the throughput. That jeopardizes any kind of weekly demo or delivery. If the team measures its WIP and its throughput, the team might decide to change its board or how it limits its WIP.
- When teams measure their cycle time, they are more likely to either right-size their work, or reduce their WIP so everyone focuses on this specific item.
- And when teams review every item's age regularly, they are more likely to reduce those items that continue to take forever.

Flow metrics create a virtuous reinforcing feedback loop. For example, when the team realizes their WIP is too high or their cycle time is too long, they will decide how to collaborate. They might not have realized that their WIP or cycle time was an outcome of too little collaboration. Now they can see the effects.

Shorter projects can help, too.

8.2.2. Plan for Shorter Projects

Software product development is about learning, not construction. So the fastest way to create a product your customers want is for the team to learn together. Here are some project techniques to use:

- After timeboxing the phases as above, create monthly releases and name them. Years ago, one of my clients broke an 18-month project into quarterly releases. The product leader realized they only needed two of those releases before the customers were satisfied.
- Or, consider monthly releases with a release train.

The shorter you can keep the up-front work, the more you will learn from the actual demos or deliveries.

8.2.3. Rolling Wave Planning to Replan

Consider the last time you planned a long trip. If you included driving, how much buffer did you give yourself, to manage the vagaries of traffic? If you included a plane flight, how much buffer did you give yourself to allow time to change planes?

Those buffer times allowed you to replan if and when something went wrong.

I'm not a fan of buffers in projects, because they have a tendency to increase when you look at them sideways. Instead, I prefer rolling wave planning.

In agile rolling wave planning, the product leader ranks the work for the next two to four weeks with the team. As the team completes this week's worth of work, the product leader plans the next week.

In a four-week plan, you might be a little "empty" at the end of the first week, before you add the fifth week's plan. But no one plans too far ahead. That flexibility allows the project much more agility.

If you're unaccustomed to rolling wave planning, I've published extensively on that topic. See the section Read My Books for More Details, just below.

Rolling wave planning helps reduce fake agility.

8.3. Reduce Fake Agility

Since I'm opposed to fake agility, we have an interesting question: How do we get agility in our current culture?

- The project reduces its unplanned feedback loops.

- The product reduces its unproven planning and learns to plan less, but more often.
- The organization focuses on the flow of the work, not on what individuals do.

Don't fall for fake agility, where individuals all start their own stories and then they need a miracle to finish the work. Hope is terrific for fiction. It's not a strategy for effective product development.

If your team is ready to explore their agility, consider this way to start with a minimum viable project: Define a product goal and the very first bit of value the customer wants. While the team learns to work together and deliver that, ask the product leader to define the next few bits of value. Then, demo the work as often as possible and release the work on a regular cadence.

Support the team as they learn from what they did. Then, they can choose one thing to improve and do it again.

You can increase your agility in any approach. It won't be easy. But the sooner the team starts to deliver value, the more management will like what you do.

That's how you can start to create a more collaborative culture. It's a virtuous, reinforcing feedback loop.

8.4. Read My Books for More Details

I've written a lot about how to use more agility in projects and the project portfolio. Read these books to see what you can do:

- Manage It! Your Guide to Modern, Pragmatic Project Management[1] focuses on replanning for all kinds of projects. In addition, there's information about how to use rolling wave planning for all projects.

---

[1] https://www.jrothman.com/manageit

- Create Your Successful Agile Project: Collaborate, Measure, Estimate, Delive[2] focuses on agile projects. That book includes chapters about how technical excellence can help the team deliver faster and rolling wave planning.
- For those of you who need to "scale" your efforts from a single project to a program of several projects, Agile and Lean Program Management: Scaling Collaboration Across the Organization[3] has suggestions for how to use these ideas for programs, including rolling wave planning.
- Manage Your Project Portfolio: Increase Your Capacity and Finish More Projects, 2nd ed[4] guides managers through agile and lean ways to manage the project portfolio to eliminate multitasking and reduce organizational WIP.
- I haven't addressed much about estimation here, but Predicting the Unpredictable: Pragmatic Approaches to Estimating Project Cost or Schedule[5] has many ideas to support a better estimation. Here's the short guidance: use cycle time.

You can design your project's approach. Decide where you need to iterate over features and release increments of value. Use the flow metrics to manage your project, regardless of your role.

Life is too short to put up with fake agility or "agile" death marches. Create a little ease and joy in your product development.

Good luck.

---

[2]https://www.jrothman.com/cysap
[3]https://www.jrothman.com/alpm
[4]https://www.jrothman.com/MYPP
[5]https://www.jrothman.com/predict

Annotated Bibliography

[BAT75] V. Basili and J. Turner, "Iterative Enhancement: A Practical Technique for Software Development," IEEE Trans. Software Eng., Dec. 1975, pp. 390- 396. Available online at https://www.cs.umd.edu/~basili/publications/journals/J04.pdf.
I will still in college when one of my professors assigned this paper. (I don't remember which professor or which class.) That's when I realized I wasn't stupid for not understanding how the product would unfold—I was normal. That, while some people could conceive of a product's architecture totally in their head, most of us needed to iterate and increment our way through the architecture and design.

[BOE86] Boehm, Barry. *A Spiral Model of Software Development and Enhancement.* Available online at https://www.cse.msu.edu/~cse435/Homework/HW3/boehm.pdf. If you read Boehm's paper, he references one of Royce's feedback visuals for the waterfall lifecycle.

[MOA13] Modig, Niklas and Pär Åhlström. *This is Lean: Resolving the Efficiency Paradox.* Rheologica Publishing, 2013. Possibly the best book about how managers should consider agile and lean. A wonderful discussion of resource efficiency vs. flow efficiency.

[MEY93] Meyer, Christopher. *Fast Cycle Time: How to Align Purpose, Strategy, and Structure for Speed.* The Free Press, New York. 1993. I read this in 1997, when a client in a regulated industry said, "What if we just finish one feature at a time? We would have complete traceability, right?" Uh, yes. The first book I read that encapsulated all the ideas behind agility at every level.

[ROT07] Rothman, Johanna. *Manage It! Your Guide to Modern, Pragmatic Project Management.* Pragmatic Bookshelf, Raleigh, NC.

2007. Read this book to become a facilitative project manager, in any lifecycle. One of the reviewers called it, "Agile for the rest of us." Learn to create an environment where the project team can thrive.

[ROT15] Rothman, Johanna. *Predicting the Unpredictable: Pragmatic Approaches to Estimating Project Cost or Schedule.* Practical Ink. 2015. Ways to think about prediction and what might make sense for you and your team. And what to do when your estimate is "wrong."

[ROT16A] Rothman, Johanna. *Agile and Lean Program Management: Scaling Collaboration Across the Organization.* Practical Ink. 2016. Scale collaboration, not process. Everything you need to know for a facilitative agile and lean approach based on principles, not practices.

[ROT16B] Rothman, Johanna. *Manage Your Project Portfolio: Increase Your Capacity and Finish More Projects, 2nd ed.* Pragmatic Bookshelf, Dallas, TX and Raleigh, NC, 2016. Sometimes, program managers encounter project portfolio decisions with the feature set, or the request for people to multitask. This book helps you manage all the work in your project portfolio. I also have more references about why multitasking is crazy in here.

[ROT17] Rothman, Johanna. *Create Your Successful Agile Project: Collaborate, Measure, Estimate, Deliver.* Pragmatic Bookshelf, Dallas, TX and Raleigh, NC, 2017. You don't need to adopt a specific framework for any given agile project. Instead, use the agile and lean principles to adjust for your project's context.

[ROT20] Rothman, Johanna. *Why Minimize Management Decision Time.* Available online at https://www.jrothman.com/wmmdt. An explanation and value stream map of the delays I see too often, just for portfolio decisions.

[ROY87] Royce, Winston. MANAGING THE DEVELOPMENT OF LARGE SOFTWARE SYSTEMS. ICSE '87: Proceedings of the 9th international conference on Software Engineering

March 1987, Pages 328–338. Available online at https://dl.acm.org/doi/10.5555/41765.41801

[SCH10] Schein, Edgar H. *Organizational Culture and Leadership.* Jossey-Bass. San Francisco 2010. Culture is not about the color of the walls or the foosball tables. Culture is about us, as humans. A fascinating look at what culture means.

[VSJ22] Vacanti, Daniel, Singh Prateek, and Colleen Johnson. *The Kanban Pocket Guide: What No One Has Told You About Kanban Could Kill You.* When teams use flow efficiency to think about how their work flows through the team, they are much more likely to create an agile approach. This short book explains how to use kanban to do so.

Glossary

Definitions for terms I've used in this book.

Backlog
  Ranked list of items that need to be completed for the product.
Behavior-Driven Development or BDD:
  Specify examples so everyone understands the story under discussion.
Flow
  The team takes a limited number of items to complete, and uses the WIP limit instead of a timebox as a way to control how much work the team takes.
Iteration
  A specific timebox, often of one to four weeks, so a team can limit the work they consider now.
Pairing
  When two people work together on one item.
Mob
  The team works all together on one item. Only one team member types (the driver), while one other team member (the navigator) takes all the input from the rest of the team (the mob). Teams often use a short timebox of five to eight minutes before everyone rotates position.
Refactor
  Cleaning the code or test while it is in development.
Servant Leadership
  An approach to managing and leading where the leader creates an environment in which people can do their best work. The leader doesn't control the work; the team does. The leader trusts the team to provide the desired results.

Sprint

> An iteration in Scrum.

Swarming

> The team works all together on one item. However, each person works according to their specific skill. The team often synchronizes every hour to see where they are. When one person is done, that person assists anyone else on the team. The one rule of swarming is this: No one starts anything new until this one item finishes.

Timebox

> A specific amount of time in which the person or team will attempt to accomplish a specific task.

WIP or Work in Progress

> Any work that is not complete.

Index

More from Johanna

People know me as the "Pragmatic Manager." I help leaders and teams see simple and reasonable alternatives that might work in their context—often with a bit of humor. Equipped with that knowledge, they can decide how to adapt how they work.

See www.jrothman.com[1] for my blogs and other writing.

If you liked this book, you might also like some of my other books[2].

Management Books:

- *Practical Ways to Manage Yourself: Modern Management Made Easy, Book 1*
- *Practical Ways to Lead and Serve—Manage—Others: Modern Management Made Easy, Book 2*
- *Practical Ways to Lead an Innovative Organization: Modern Management Made Easy, Book 3*
- *Behind Closed Doors: Secrets of Great Management*
- *Hiring Geeks That Fit*

Product Development:

- *From Chaos to Successful Distributed Agile Teams: Collaborate to Deliver*
- *Create Your Successful Agile Project: Collaborate, Measure, Estimate, Deliver*
- *Manage Your Project Portfolio: Increase Your Capacity and Finish More Projects, 2nd ed*

---

[1]https://www.jrothman.com
[2]https://www.jrothman.com/books/

- *Agile and Lean Program Management: Scaling Collaboration Across the Organization*
- *Diving for Hidden Treasures: Uncovering the Cost of Delay Your Project Portfolio*
- *Predicting the Unpredictable: Pragmatic Approaches to Estimating Project Cost or Schedule*
- *Project Portfolio Tips: Twelve Ideas for Focusing on the Work You Need to Start & Finish*
- *Manage It!: Your Guide to Modern, Pragmatic Project Management*

Personal Development:

- *Successful Independent Consulting*
- *Free Your Inner Nonfiction Writer*
- *Write a Conference Proposal*
- *Manage Your Job Search*

I'd like to stay in touch with you. If you don't already subscribe, please sign up for my email newsletter, the Pragmatic Manager[3]. Once a month, I send content you can use, plus announcements of workshops and more.

I'm on the various social media:

- LinkedIn: https://www.linkedin.com/in/johannarothman)
- X/Twitter: @johannarothman
- Mastodon: https://mastodon.sdf.org/@johannarothman
- YouTube: https://www.youtube.com/@johannarothman

Did this book help you? If so, please consider writing a review of it. Reviews help other readers find books. Thanks!

Johanna

---

[3]https://www.jrothman.com/pragmaticmanager/

www.ingramcontent.com/pod-product-compliance
Lightning Source LLC
Chambersburg PA
CBHW071141050326
40690CB00008B/1524